DRAMA AND WRITING AGES 5-11

Drama and Writing Ages 5-11 is a practical guide for teachers to develop and inspire writing through using drama in the classroom. Each of the ten chapters provides step-by-step guidance and creative prompts for writing that apply to both key stage one and key stage two, enabling teachers to motivate their pupils by creating meaningful contexts, audiences and purposes to encourage writing. With a wide range of ideas to apply to the classroom, from simple classroom strategies to more complex units of work, this book is suitable for all teachers – including those who hold limited experience of using drama in the classroom.

Including key definitions of drama strategies and practical advice to apply to the classroom, the chapters are presented in two parts:

- Part I provides short and simple drama strategies to act as a helping hand, stimulating the focus of a writing lesson.
- Part II provides longer dramatic contexts with a compelling sense of audience and purpose, including a range of opportunities for writing. These prompts may span two or more lessons.

Drama and Writing Ages 5-11 is an essential read for any primary school teacher seeking practical strategies to incorporate drama into the classroom, teaching the craft of writing in a creative, fun and meaningful way.

Larraine S. Harrison is a former primary school teacher and local authority school improvement adviser. She holds many years of experience running national CPD courses on drama in education. Currently, she works as a consultant for drama in education, a school governor and a children's author.

DRAMA AND WRITING AGES 5-11

A Practical Book of Ideas for Primary Teachers

Larraine S. Harrison

Designed cover image: © Getty Images

First published 2023
by Routledge
4 Park Square, Milton Park, Abingdon, Oxon OX14 4RN

and by Routledge
605 Third Avenue, New York, NY 10158

Routledge is an imprint of the Taylor & Francis Group, an informa business

© 2023 Larraine Harrison

The right of Larraine Harrison to be identified as author of this work has been asserted in accordance with sections 77 and 78 of the Copyright, Designs and Patents Act 1988.

All rights reserved. No part of this book may be reprinted or reproduced or utilised in any form or by any electronic, mechanical, or other means, now known or hereafter invented, including photocopying and recording, or in any information storage or retrieval system, without permission in writing from the publishers.

Trademark notice: Product or corporate names may be trademarks or registered trademarks, and are used only for identification and explanation without intent to infringe.

British Library Cataloguing-in-Publication Data
A catalogue record for this book is available from the British Library

Library of Congress Cataloging-in-Publication Data
Names: Harrison, Larraine S., author.
Title: Drama and writing ages 5-11 : a practical book of ideas for primary teachers / Larraine S. Harrison.
Description: Abingdon, Oxon ; New York, NY : Routledge, 2023.
Identifiers: LCCN 2022045839 (print) | LCCN 2022045840 (ebook) | ISBN 9781032325866 (hardback) | ISBN 9781032325880 (paperback) | ISBN 9781003315742 (ebook)
Subjects: LCSH: Composition (Language arts)--Study and teaching (Primary) | English language--Composition and exercises--Study and teaching (Primary) | Drama in education--Study and teaching (Primary)
Classification: LCC LB1576 .H259 2023 (print) | LCC LB1576 (ebook) | DDC 372.6--dc23/eng/20221123
LC record available at https://lccn.loc.gov/2022045839
LC ebook record available at https://lccn.loc.gov/2022045840

ISBN: 978-1-032-32586-6 (hbk)
ISBN: 978-1-032-32588-0 (pbk)
ISBN: 978-1-003-31574-2 (ebk)

DOI: 10.4324/9781003315742

Typeset in Interstate
by KnowledgeWorks Global Ltd.

CONTENTS

Acknowledgements   vii

Drama and writing: Introduction   1

PART I: DRAMA AS A HELPING HAND   7

1 Physical theatre   9
   The pathway   9
   Embodied capital letters (key stage one)   15
   The punctuation line up   17

2 Freezing the narrative   22
   Plot books   22
   Flashbacks, flash-forward and dreams   25
   Eyewitnesses   26
   Writing in the frame   26

3 Strange hot-seating   27
   Real creatures   28
   Imaginary creatures   30
   Objects and the environment   33

4 Viewpoints   37
   Balanced arguments and opinions   37
      Cats versus dogs   38
      Views on zoos   39
      The discussion book   43
   Character viewpoints: Diaries, letters and postcards   45

5 Bubbles, comics and playscripts   46
   An extra frame   46
   The one-minute playscript (key stage two)   53
   Silent movie scripts   58

6 Write back   60
   Write back key stage one examples   61
      Goldilocks and the Three Bears   62
      The Three Little Pigs   64

Further suggestions — 66
   The Three Billy Goats Gruff — 66
   The Owl Who Was Afraid of the Dark by Jill Tomlinson — 66
Write back key stage two examples — 66
   Dog in the Playground by Allan Ahlberg — 67
   Matilda by Hilaire Belloc — 70
Further suggestions — 73
   Beowulf by Charles Keeping and Kevin Crossley Holland — 73
   Lightning Falls by Amy Wilson — 73
   Mr Wolf's Class by Aron Nels Steinke — 73

PART II: DRAMA AS A COMPELLING CONTEXT — 75

7 An imaginary community: Key stage one and lower key stage two — 77
Key stage one example: Pets corner — 78
Key stage one/lower key stage two example: A beautiful place — 80

8 An imaginary community: Upper key stage two — 88
Upper key stage two example 1: A village under threat — 89
Upper key stage two example 2: A historical community — 96
Mantle of the expert — 100

9 An imaginary journey — 101
Key stage one examples — 102
Key stage two example: The expedition — 105

10 Open-ended drama — 110
Key stage one examples — 111
   a *The letter* — 111
   b *The door* — 112
   c *The special box* — 113
   d *Dramatic play* — 114
Key stage two examples — 115
   a *The key* — 115
   b *Directing the story* — 116

Conclusion — 118

Drama strategies — 121

Further reading and resources — 130

ACKNOWLEDGEMENTS

I would like to thank all the teachers who have sent me children's written work based on drama and all the children who have made both the drama and the writing so vivid and memorable. Thanks also to Claire Davies and Jane Simpkins of Waterton Academy Trust for their professional advice and encouragement and to the team at Routledge.

Finally, thanks to my husband Martyn and my family for their continual practical and emotional support.

Drama and writing
Introduction

What is this book about and who is it for?

This book is about how to use drama to support the teaching of writing in the primary school. Its purpose is twofold: (1) to encourage teachers to use drama as a stimulus and meaningful context for writing and (2) to raise awareness of the potential of drama as a learning medium. It is not a book about how to teach writing but rather a book about how to provide engaging activities and contexts that offer a range of audiences and purposes for writing.

The book is for all primary teachers including ITT students and other educators with limited knowledge and understanding of drama and its potential to support writing.

The book is divided into two parts:

Part I: Drama as a Helping Hand focuses on simple drama strategies which provide a helping hand in the writing classroom. These approaches use drama to stimulate or illustrate a particular aspect of writing.

Part II: Drama as a Compelling Context focuses on one or more drama lessons where imaginary contexts provide compelling audiences and purposes for writing.

Each idea is explained via separate examples for key stages one and two where appropriate.

Definitions of the drama strategies referred to in the book are provided for further clarification.

Suggestions for resources and further reading are included for those who wish to extend their knowledge and understanding of drama as a learning medium.

Why use drama for writing

Real-life experiences can provide many opportunities for writing but can be difficult to organise on a regular basis. However, drama can provide a wealth of experiences for writing, both real and imagined because, although drama is an imaginary experience, it is the tangible enactment of that experience that helps children with recall and response when writing.

How to manage drama: Setting the ground rules

Since drama in education is a cross-curricular learning tool, it is managed in the same way regardless of the subject area, whether that be reading for meaning or writing. Readers will therefore find similar advice in my sister book: *Drama and Reading for Meaning Ages 4-11* (Routledge, 2022).

The drama contract

Drama is unique in that it involves taking an active part in a fictional world, whilst at the same time being grounded in reality. Children taking part in drama straddle the line between fiction and reality, moving between the two worlds with relative ease. For drama to occur, children need to agree to behave as if they were somewhere else, somebody else or something else. This agreement is known as **The Drama Contract**. It may be informal or formal, explicit or implicit, but whatever form it takes, the drama contract is crucial to the success of the drama process. Confusion about expectations can undermine the drama process, leading to disengagement and frustration.

The way in which the contract is introduced will depend on the age and confidence of the children and the context of the drama. For very young children, the contract may take the form of a more implicit exchange. For example:

Excuse me Giants, can you show me how you walk with big steps?

By assuming the children are giants, the teacher is in effect inviting the children to accept the pretence. If the children then respond by walking like giants, they are implicitly agreeing to accept the pretence.

However, young children also understand when the contract is made more explicit. For example:

When we start our story/drama, we need to pretend we are giants walking around with big steps. Can we do that?

Older children respond best to a more explicit approach to the contract using language more appropriate to their age group. For example:

For this drama activity I need you to take on the roles of/play the parts of/imagine you are... the villagers in the story. Will that be OK?

Drama is closely linked to play and most children are keen to take part if the contract is presented in a positive way that assumes co-operation. However, there may be occasions when a child appears anxious or is reluctant to agree. This is more likely to occur if they are new to drama work. The way you respond depends on your knowledge of the child but an invitation to observe until the child feels more comfortable or able to accept the pretence is often all that is required. When children see others enjoying the drama, they usually opt to accept the contract and join in.

Defining the space

Unless you are working in a drama studio, the room you are in will likely include areas and items that you do not wish children to access during the drama. In this case, it's important to define the drama space before you begin, so children are clear about any areas and items that are out of bounds.

Stopping and starting

Use clear signals for stopping and starting the drama, such as the words *Action* and *Freeze*. You can use different sounds instead of these words, but whatever you choose needs to be used consistently, so you can manage the drama process at all times.

Time to think

Children cannot produce their best work if they are given insufficient time to think and prepare for a task and this also applies to drama. Clear instructions with time to think are key to the management of a drama lesson and are particularly important for children with special or additional needs. There are occasions when a spontaneous response is required, but children should be warned beforehand if this is the case, and support given to those who may struggle.

Choosing the best drama strategy

Your choice of strategy is an important factor in the successful management of the drama. The choice will depend on a number of considerations including the learning objective and the needs and confidence of the particular group of children, but another important consideration is your own level of confidence and experience in drama. Start with what you are comfortable with and build your repertoire of drama strategies one step at a time.

Inclusion

Whilst most children in mainstream schools are able and willing to take part in drama activities, there may be times when adaptations are needed to ensure all children are given an opportunity to participate. Ensuring instructions are simple and clear with not too many challenges at one go, together with allowing children plenty of time to think, plan and respond during the drama are particularly important for those who need more processing time. Other adaptations include more practical adjustments like making sure the space is adequate for all children to take part and including pictures or symbols wherever possible.

If the children are new to drama, some may need more time to adjust than others or may struggle with the idea of taking on a role. If this is the case they should be allowed to observe until they feel comfortable or offered an observational role such as an artist, note-taking journalist or documentary maker recording some of the experience on video. Younger children often like to take on roles like the keeper of any props, the timekeeper or the teacher's helper.

There are other occasions when the opposite occurs. A child will take on a role with such enthusiasm that they want to continue to play that same role in subsequent dramas, no matter what the context. This can be challenging but can sometimes be accommodated by suggesting the role has different characteristics or performs different tasks each time. If this situation occurs, be as flexible as you can and try not to draw attention to it.

Some children take on roles willingly but find the transition out of that role difficult to handle. Activities such as waving an imaginary wand to make the character disappear or pretending to take off an imaginary invisible character costume can help younger children, whilst older children benefit from having plenty of time to reflect out of role.

Whether children are cautious or enthusiastic, helping them to understand and be reassured that drama is about pretence and not reality is crucial. For some children, this may need to be quietly reaffirmed several times during the drama until they become used to the idea.

Many children with special and additional needs excel within a dramatic context, leading to improved levels of self-esteem and confidence within the group.

Frequently asked questions

Do we need a large space for drama?

The short answer is no. Many drama strategies can take place in the classroom, without the need to move the furniture. Some undoubtedly work best in a cleared or larger space, but if necessary these can be adapted to the classroom environment. Where a drama involves a sequence of lessons it's often useful to use a larger space for the first lesson, with subsequent lessons taking place in the classroom.

How do I keep control of a lively class during a drama lesson?

Drama in education is a very structured approach to learning. Whilst it gives children a certain amount of freedom, it also requires the setting of clear boundaries and expectations. Start with the contract, define the space and be consistent with your expectations. Most children are keen to abide by the rules if the reasons for them are explained and a quiet word to any individual child who breaks them is often all that is required. If there are problems with several children, stop the drama immediately, explain the problem and re-negotiate. Be prepared to do this as many times as it takes until they become used to the expectations. This may be tough at first but children are usually keen to take part in drama and most will be prepared to respect the ground rules if they are explained clearly and applied consistently.

Choose a drama strategy that both you and the children will be comfortable with. If working in drama will be a new experience for everyone, start with a structured activity like a whole class freeze-frame, moving on to more ambitious approaches like whole group drama when you feel more confident.

Making your drama sufficiently engaging is also important when teaching a lively group, but every class is different, and if you feel the drama isn't engaging the children, be prepared to stop. Try to find out what went wrong, either from the children and/or from reflecting on the lesson afterwards and ask yourself if there was anything you could have done to engage the children more effectively before trying again.

How can I fit drama into an already crowded curriculum?

Where drama is used as a teaching tool, as in this book, it becomes a means to an end, rather than a discreet subject requiring extra time. The drama strategies themselves also vary in the time they take to complete. If time is a problem, start with one of the shorter activities and build up your repertoire, so drama becomes an integral part of your teaching toolkit. You will find the impact is well worth the time invested.

I'm not good at acting, so how can I use drama to teach?

Drama as a teaching method does not require great acting skills. Whilst teacher-in-role is an excellent strategy and one I would recommend you work towards, it is not essential for every drama strategy. You can achieve a similar outcome via an imaginary letter or message from a character. Alternatively, you can employ the skills of another more confident member of staff such as a teaching assistant if appropriate. The important thing is for adults to approach their roles with integrity, modelling and presenting drama to the children as a legitimate way of learning.

Do children need to warm up with a drama game before taking part in drama?

Drama games are valuable but they are not like other games. There are no winners and losers. They are designed to develop children's personal, emotional and social skills and can make a valuable contribution to learning. They are often used by high school drama teachers as warm-ups for improvisation work or theatre. However, in primary schools, unless they make a significant contribution to the theme of the drama, they are best carried out in a separate lesson. It is rarely practical to use warm-ups where drama forms an integral part of a literacy lesson and it can be challenging to introduce a drama about a serious issue after a lively game.

If the drama is introduced in a structured way where children are given time to think and prepare, there is less need for a warm-up.

PART I
Drama as a Helping Hand

1 Physical theatre

Opportunities for writing

KS1 *Composing appropriate words to describe a setting; forming phrases into simple sentences; combining and sequencing sentences to form a narrative; using simple adjectives and prepositions; reading aloud chorally; using capital letters for names of people and places; identifying and using a full stop, question mark and exclamation mark to conclude a sentence.*

KS2 *Selecting genre-appropriate vocabulary for a setting; turning phrases into sentences and sentences into a paragraph; using double adjectives and prepositions; reading written work aloud to convey meaning; placing commas, speech marks and other punctuation into complex sentences.*

Contents	
The pathway	9
Embodied capital letters (key stage one)	15
The punctuation line up	17

Drama strategies

The pathway and other forms of physical theatre
Teacher-in-role/toy-in-role

The pathway

This drama strategy involves small groups of children using their bodies to create obstacles or features along a pathway for a character to walk along. Each group creates one part of the pathway along with a phrase to indicate where the character has to walk at that point e.g. *through a dark wood*. The order of the obstacles is selected with a reader/audience in mind, as if structuring a paragraph. As a teacher-in-role or a toy moved by the teacher negotiates the different parts of the pathway, the groups say their phrases out loud. After the drama, the phrases are written down, adding additional words such as verbs and prepositions to form sentences describing the character's journey. These sentences are then recorded as a list. The list is then redrafted and reorganised to form a flowing composite paragraph based on the journey of the character through the pathway setting.

The creation and embodiment of a story setting through physical theatre provides a visual representation and an opportunity for discussion, which supports subsequent writing. It also creates a sense of ownership and commitment to the end product. The drama creates an opportunity for older children to learn how to write a setting using a variety of prepositions and double adjectives and illustrates the difference between a phrase and a sentence and a list of sentences and a smoothly flowing paragraph. The following examples illustrate two of the many ways in which the pathway can provide an opportunity to stimulate writing.

KEY STAGE ONE EXAMPLE: TEDDY'S WALK

Links to reading

ROSIE'S WALK by Pat Hutchins
WALKING THROUGH THE JUNGLE by Julie Lacome
WE'RE GOING ON A BEAR HUNT by Michael Rosen

Planning and resources

You will need

- Sufficient space for children to stand opposite each other in two lines to form a physical pathway;
- A Teddy or similar figure;
- A large screen for composite writing and writing materials;
- Display space for the story and illustrations and materials for children to create the illustrations;
- (Optional) A simple device to make a short audio recording.

What to do

- Introduce the Teddy. Ask the children to help you write a story called Teddy's Walk, about a Teddy who went for a walk in the countryside.
- Tell the children that you know how the story starts but that is all. Write the title and the first few words on the board and then ask the children to read it back with you e.g. TEDDY'S WALK. *One day Teddy went for a walk in the countryside. He went...*
- Ask the children if they will help you imagine what Teddy's walk was like by making the path with their bodies. To demonstrate this, ask two children to make a bridge with their bodies such as holding hands to make an arch. Then walk the Teddy over their bridge saying *Teddy went over a bridge.*

Physical theatre 11

- If appropriate, ask the children to think of a word/adjective to describe the bridge e.g. *wooden, wobbly*. Add this to the sentence and repeat the bridge example saying the new sentence.
- Talk about where else Teddy could walk by suggesting simple prepositions e.g. *over, under, round, between, up, down* or *through* and then talk about how pairs might represent these with their bodies. Some children may need a few examples such as lying down with hands outstretched in a rippling movement to represent a narrow stream for Teddy to walk over, etc. Once children understand the concept, organise them into pairs or threes and ask each group to think of and practise making one part of the pathway with their bodies. Stress that whatever they choose, you must be able to walk the Teddy along their pathway. Most children are able to grasp this idea, but if some children are struggling to grasp this idea, you can build up the pathway with them one pair at a time as a whole class activity.
- Ask each group to be ready to tell everyone where Teddy walked when he came to their part of the pathway e.g. *over a wobbly bridge/across slippery stepping stones/up a steep hill/along a muddy path*. Make a note of their descriptions as they share them with the class before the drama. This allows you to offer support and can be used to remind them in the drama.
- Once each group has decided on how to arrange their bodies into a physical shape and created a phrase, ask them to organise themselves into the pathway for Teddy to walk along. Whether you allow the groups to work out the order of the features for themselves or direct the procedure will depend on the confidence and social health of the class. If children's concentration levels permit, ask if there is a preferred order of the features to make the story more interesting. For example, there may be similar things that would be better separated, or the most exciting thing may be better at the end, etc. This is a way of asking children to verbally structure a narrative paragraph with a reader in mind.
- Narrate your way into the action by saying *This is the story of Teddy's Walk. One day Teddy went for a walk in the countryside. He went...* Walk the Teddy through each section, pausing before each one to ask that group *Where did Teddy go next?* The children should describe Teddy's journey through their part of the pathway aloud each time. Repeat their words to add status and enable other children to hear but rephrase them as a sentence each time e.g. *through a dark wood* becomes *He went through a dark wood*.
- Speak Teddy's thoughts aloud as he negotiates each section e.g. *This bridge is very wobbly, I hope I don't fall off*. These thoughts help sustain concentration, add status to the children's ideas and model a character's response to a setting.
- Arrange the children in front of the board and ask them to help you remember the sequence of Teddy's walk. Record it visually in some way, either as a map, simple drawings or symbols.

Writing the sentences

By this point, every child will have co-created and physically represented one part of Teddy's Walk, along with a verbal description visually recorded on the board. This creates a sense of ownership and responsibility for turning their phrase into a good sentence in order to contribute to the story. How this is developed depends on the age and needs of the children. Here is one suggestion:

- Work as a whole class to convert the phrases into a list of sentences and then craft and sequence them into a story using connectives and personal pronouns where appropriate.
- Then ask them to make the pathway again, so you can read the final story as you move Teddy along the path. The story can be read from a paper copy in your hand or from the board if you can see it clearly.

'Publishing' the writing

- Sit the children together in the place they usually listen to stories and ask them to listen to their story about Teddy's Walk.
- After the reading, speculate and ask questions such as: *Who thinks the story is good enough to go on our wall? I wonder which was your favourite part/the most difficult part of Teddy's Walk and why you think that – tell a partner.*
- Display the children's story on the wall. If space permits, it can be displayed as a horizontal line of separate sentences to reflect the walk, like different pages of a picture book. Illustrations can be created and displayed above and below or around each sentence as appropriate.
- Once the story has been 'published' as a display, suggest that the class read it to Teddy along with you. If appropriate, talk briefly about how best to read certain parts. Teddy listens carefully and loves the story so much that he jumps up and down with delight.
- If possible, invite another member of staff who hasn't read the story to read the display and ask for feedback. Children usually love to tell an adult audience which particular part of the story they created.
- (Optional) Make a recording of Teddy's Walk as if it were an audiobook and play it back to the children asking them if they enjoyed it and if you read it clearly, etc. If you have a facility for individual children to listen to recordings of stories, this recording can be added to the stories already available.

Extension activities

- Confident writers may like to work individually or in small teacher-led groups to write another version of a Walk using a different toy or a different setting.
- Talk, draw and write about what happened next in the story.
- Talk about and write a new beginning where we find out why Teddy went for the walk or consider other possibilities such as someone secretly following or chasing Teddy.

KEY STAGE TWO EXAMPLE: PERSON UNKNOWN

Links to reading

TOM'S MIDNIGHT GARDEN (Chapter 3) by Phillipa Pearce
THE LONG WAY HOME by Sophie Kirtley
THE LONGEST NIGHT OF CHARLIE MOON by Christopher Edge
LAND OF ROAR by Jenny McLachlan
THE CASTLE OF TANGLED MAGIC by Sophie Anderson

Planning and resources

You will need

- Sufficient space for children to stand in two lines opposite each other in a curved or twisted shape.
- A plain scarf or similar item to represent a character.
- A large sheet of paper or screen area.
- A recording device to record the start of an imaginary audiobook.
- A sign saying SILENCE – ON AIR.

What to do

Creating the setting

- Ask the children to work with you to compose the opening paragraph of a story that you intend to record as if for an audiobook. Explain that the function of this paragraph is to introduce and create interest in the setting and the main character. Explain that the story starts with a mysterious unknown character walking along a challenging pathway across the countryside. The character is called Person Unknown.
- Write the start of the paragraph on the board e.g. *Person Unknown took a deep breath. The pathway ahead was going to be a challenge.*
- Ask the children to help visualise the setting by using Physical Theatre, where pairs or groups use their bodies to represent the different features of the pathway. Explain that you will represent Person Unknown walking the pathway, so the features must be large enough for you to physically pass along it.
- Talk about what words in the first sentences tell us about the nature of the pathway and how Person Unknown feels about the prospect. Point out the phrase *took a deep breath* as an example of 'Show Not Tell' revealing a character's emotions.
- Ask the class to decide on a genre for this story as this will affect their choices e.g. a sci-fi story or a horror story will need different features for the pathway than a real-life adventure.
- As an example of the physical theatre, ask two children to make a bridge shape for you to walk under by joining hands to make an archway. Collect suggestions about other ways to make the route more interesting e.g. join hands along the floor for the character to step over a bubbling stream, stand together in twisted shapes as large trees with poisonous leaves for them to walk through or tall boulders for them to squeeze between, etc.

- Arrange the children into pairs or threes and allow them time to create and practise making their part of the pathway. They also need to compose a short description of what Person Unknown sees or experiences as they negotiate their part of the pathway. This needs to be appropriate for the chosen genre e.g. *a low wooden bridge with spiders hanging down* might be appropriate for a horror story.
- Ask each group to select one person to call out their descriptive phrase as Person Unknown approaches.
- Now ask the groups to make the pathway with their bodies. Allow them to decide on the order in which they place themselves. Then ask whether there is enough variety for a reader in the order in which the challenges are presented e.g. *are there too many similar challenges placed together?* Go with what the majority of the class feels and reorder the sequence if necessary.
- Ask groups to make the pathway in the agreed order.
- Explain that you will use the scarf as a sign of role to play the part of the Person Unknown. You will stop before each part of the pathway to allow one of that group to describe out loud what the character is about to negotiate e.g. *twisted black trees; ice-bound stepping stones*. Explain that you will repeat the phrase each time so everyone can hear.
- Using the words *Action* and *Freeze* to start and stop the drama, put on the scarf and walk the pathway, repeating the descriptive phrases each time.

Drafting the writing

Move back to sitting at the tables and ask groups to turn their phrases into sentences and then work on them to make them more interesting. The work can go in a number of different directions from this point, depending on the needs of the children and the learning objectives. Potential areas to focus on include the following:

- Form a sentence using double adjectives to describe the pathway such as a gnarled, twisted tree, etc.
- After agreeing on a personal pronoun for Person Unknown (*he, she or they*) and a tense for the story, use interesting verbs and adverbs to create a sentence describing how the character might move through each section of the pathway or what they might sense e.g. *Deafened by the sound of rushing water, she stepped carefully over the slippery stepping stones.* Or explore ways to indicate the character's emotional responses to the setting in a 'Show Not Tell' manner.

'Publishing' the writing

- Remind the children that you intend to record this opening paragraph as if it were the start of an audiobook.
- On a shared board, collect and write the sentences for the opening of the story.
- Read the sentences aloud to the children and talk about how they could turn the list of sentences into a flowing, cohesive paragraph e.g. by adding connectives or rearranging words, etc. Redraft according to the children's suggestions. Then read aloud again, asking if it is now suitable for the audiobook.

- Ask children's advice on how to read particular parts of the written work to give readers' clues about the setting and atmosphere you want to create e.g. how to read with appropriate tone in different parts.
- After a rehearsal for the children's approval, put up the sign saying On Air and record the reading.
- Playback the reading and ask for comments, adapting and re-recording if necessary.

Extension activities

- Ask the children to compose their own audiobook paragraphs of 5 or 6 lines describing a character travelling through a setting in a particular genre. Reinforce the need to be able to read their paragraph aloud with the appropriate tone to convey meaning. Some children may prefer another child or a teacher to read out their paragraph in the way actors read audiobooks for authors, but if this is the case they should advise on how it is to be read. The paragraphs can be read aloud as if for an imaginary audiobook during teacher-led group work, or they can be recorded.
- Suggestions for a new pathway setting might include the following: corridors in a spooky house or a magical castle, a pathway to a sci-fi world: an underground passageway; a challenge for a charity/reality TV game show.
- Ask the class to help you rewrite some or the entire audio paragraph in a different tense and assess the impact. Compare the effect to the tense used in the audiobook.

Embodied capital letters (key stage one)

This short-fun activity for key stage one involves pairs of children making capital letters with their bodies. It helps consolidate the shapes for early writers and reinforces the use of capitals when writing the days of the week and the names of people and places.

Links to reading

>MY NAME IS... by Pauline Clarke (from *The Booktime Book of Fantastic First Poems* Ed. June Crebbin)

Planning and resources

You will need

- A hall or cleared space where children can lie on the floor.
- A large alphabet chart of capital and lower case letters.
- A list of the days of the week.
- Whiteboards and pens for the children.

What to do

- Display the alphabet chart and the list of days of the week.
- Explain that days of the week always start with a capital letter and to help us remember this, we are going to see if we can make the capital letter shapes of these words with our bodies. Ask a child to come to the front and demonstrate how you can make the letter M for Monday by standing side by side with arms bent sideways to form the V shape. Then ask for two children to show how they could make the capital T for Tuesday in a similar way. This is more difficult, so suggest how they might complete it by lying on the floor.
- Repeat this with the other days of the week.
- Explain to the children that capital letters are also used for the first letter of people's names. Provide some examples using the children's own names, including middle names if appropriate. Ask them to work in pairs to write down both their names on a whiteboard and hold them up so you can check they all start with capital letters.
- Select one child with a different initial from the ones used for the days of the week. Ask them to come to the front with their partner and their name boards. Then working with these children and suggestions from the class, allow them to demonstrate how they might make the shape of one of their initials using their bodies e.g. the letter H can be represented by standing facing each other and joining your outstretched hands in the middle. Some letters are easier to represent on the floor such as the letter D that would be one child lying on the floor in a straight line and the other curving over them either standing up or beside them on the floor. Go through a few more challenging initials in the class such as B, J, R and talk about and/or demonstrate how these might be represented.
- When you feel children understand the task, ask pairs to take their whiteboards with their names on them and find a space in the hall. Ask them to use their bodies to make the capital letters for the start of both children's first and last names i.e. four letters, or just their first names. They should then choose one letter to show the class.
- Ask each pair to tell everyone what and whose letter they intend to perform before they share it with the class. Make constant reference to the way the capital letters are constructed and refer to the chart if necessary.
- If appropriate, repeat the process with the names of familiar people and places.

'Publishing/performing' the writing

- Children in the class use their bodies to create the shapes of upper and lower case letters to form a sentence. This can be photographed to make a poster or notice e.g. Welcome to ... (add the name of the school with the capital letters in the correct place).

Extension activities

- Repeat the activity with the names of characters from familiar stories.
- Browse a big book with the class to spot the capital letters used for characters' names.

The punctuation line up

In this activity, children perform movements representing punctuation marks, placing them within a sentence represented by a line of children holding word cards at the front of the class. The aim is to support ongoing work on punctuation recognition and its placement within a sentence in a fun and visually stimulating way.

Use the actions as a guide as shown in Figure 1.1 or invent new ones.

Full stop: *stamp one foot.*
Question mark: *make the arched shape of the top of the question mark by curving both arms above the head. Stand straight to represent the stem and make a small jump with both feet to represent the dot underneath.*
Exclamation mark: *stand straight and put both arms in the air with palms together to represent the stem. Make a small jump with feet together to represent the dot underneath.*
Comma: *take one step diagonally and sway slightly to and fro.*

Opening speech marks   Closing speech marks   Exclamation mark (and one jump for dot)   Question mark (and one jump for dot)

Figure 1.1 Drawings by Esther Campbell

Opening speech marks: *turn sideways towards the first spoken word. Arch both arms above the head of the child holding this word, to make the shape of inverted commas.*
Closing speech marks: *turn sideways facing the last spoken word. Arch both arms above the head of the child holding this word, to make the shape of inverted commas.*
Colon: *make two fists one directly above the other at waist height.*
Semi-colon: *make the bottom comma as above, whilst making a fist with one hand at waist height.*
Apostrophe: *raise a curved hand in the air.*

KEY STAGE ONE EXAMPLE: FULL STOPS, QUESTION MARKS AND EXCLAMATION MARKS

Links to reading

THE PERFECT PUNCTUATION BOOK by Kate Petty

The following two books are examples of many others with repeated use of question marks and exclamation marks:

(Question marks) *ODD SOCKS* by Neal Zetter
(Exclamation marks) *FARMER DUCK* by Martin Waddell

Planning and resources

You will need

- A hall or cleared space
- Blank cards or whiteboards and pens
- Enough whiteboards or cards with single words on to make up a simple sentence. Choose one from a familiar story or make one up e.g. *Sam wants some toast*.
- A display board or screen in the classroom where every child can see it, including those standing at the front of the class.

What to do

- In a hall or cleared area, ask the children to find a space. Explain that when you say Go, they should walk around the room in any direction without touching anyone else. When you say the words *Full Stop* and hold up the card with the full stop written on it, they should stamp their feet and come to a stop. Remind them that this full stop mark is how they usually end a sentence. Repeat the activity.
- Explain that there is another way of signalling a stop at the end of a sentence and that is when you are asking a question. Ask a child to write a large question mark on a whiteboard. Hold up the question mark card and explain that they should move again on the word Go, but if you call out *Question Mark*, they should stop and make the shape of a question mark.
- Repeat this a few times with both a question mark and a full stop before introducing an exclamation mark as another way to end a sentence.

Physical theatre

- Repeat with all three at different times until the children are familiar with the moves.
- Back in the classroom, write each word of your chosen sentence on a whiteboard, minus any punctuation marks. Give the boards to individual children to hold in front of them at waist height in a line at the front of the class.
- Point to each word in the sentence in turn and ask the class to read it aloud with you. Insist the children only say the word when you point to it.
- Write the same sentence on a display board or screen where every child can see it, including those at the front of the class.
- Ask the children to tell you what punctuation mark is missing or what is missing at the end of the sentence. Ask a child to stand in the line of words in the place where that punctuation mark would be located e.g. in the sentence *Sam wants some toast* the child representing the full stop would stand at the end of the line after the child holding the word *toast*.
- Ask the children to read the sentence again as you point to the words, but when you point to the full stop they should say *Full Stop*. The child representing the full stop should then stamp one of their feet as in the movement activity.
- Add a full stop to the sentence on the board, asking the children to check it is in the right place.
- Take away some of the words and add new ones to turn the sentence into a question e.g. *Sam wants some toast* becomes **Does** Sam **want** some toast.
- Write this sentence on the display board.
- Ask the children if there would be a different punctuation mark at the end of this new sentence and why. Ask the child representing the full stop to sit down and replace their position with another child to represent the question mark using the movement they learnt in the hall activity.
- Read the sentence again in the same way as before i.e. when you point to the child representing the question mark they should name it and the child should perform the action.
- Add the punctuation mark to the new sentence on the board.
- Change the words in the sentence to reflect a situation with potential for an exclamation mark e.g. *Sam threw away his toast* and repeat the process.
- The focus here is on the fact that a question mark and an exclamation mark replace a full stop at the end of a sentence.

'Publishing/performing' the writing

Ask the children to perform a punctuation line up for an assembly, using a sentence linked to a topic or from a familiar story.

KEY STAGE TWO EXAMPLE: SPEECH MARKS AND OTHER PUNCTUATION

Links to reading

(Apostrophes) *THE GIRLS LIKE SPAGHETTI* by Lynne Truss
TRICKY PUNCTUATION IN CARTOONS by Lidia Stanton

QUESTION MARK by Michael Rosen
THE INTERRUPTING FULL STOP by Coral Rumble

Planning and resources

You will need

- One or two sentences with potential for a number of punctuation marks, including direct speech e.g. a sentence such as *I hate toast said Sam but I like bread* allows a conversation about the positioning of the speech marks and where the comma should go. Make up a sentence to suit your needs or use a sentence or verse from a text which uses different punctuation e.g. **Q FOR A POEM by Michael Rosen** (*Jelly Boots, Smelly Boots*, Bloomsbury 2016);
- Word cards or small whiteboards, one for every word in your chosen sentence;
- A few blank whiteboards or cards and a thick pen;
- Sufficient space at the front of the class for the children holding the word cards to stand in a line. This can be a curved line if space is tight;
- A display board or screen where all children can see it, including those at the front of the class.

What to do

- Teach the children the actions for the punctuation marks in your chosen sentence.
- Distribute the word cards or whiteboards amongst a group of children and ask them to stand in a line with their boards in front of them to form a sentence.
- Ask the class to read the words of the sentence in chorus as you point to each one in turn.
- Write the sentence on a display board or screen where all the children can see it.
- Ask the class if they can spot one missing punctuation mark from this sentence. Then invite the child who made the first suggestion to stand in the line in the place where that mark would appear e.g. a full stop in the sentence *I hate toast said Sam but I do like bread* would mean the child should stand after the word *bread* but not after the word *toast*. The class can direct this child beforehand if more appropriate.
- Add the punctuation mark to the written version on the board, asking the children to check whether it goes in the correct place.
- Perform the other punctuation marks with the same sentence or sentences in the same way. If your sentence includes an apostrophe within a word, you will need to rewrite the word as two cards, to make room for the child performing the action e.g. *the dog s basket*.

'Publishing/performing' the writing

- Ask children to write a large version of the sentence on a display board or screen, using different colours for the different types of marks.

- Perform a punctuation line up in an assembly with a sentence linked to a relevant topic and video it for the class to view again later if appropriate.

Extension activity

The Punctuation Challenge: Ask pairs to browse texts to find a sentence with punctuation that they think would challenge the class. They should copy out the original with the correct punctuation and hide it before writing the individual words on cards or whiteboards for the class to perform. They then reveal their secret sentence to check if the rest of the class have met the challenge.

2 Freezing the narrative

Opportunities for writing

Plots, key moments, story structures, writing in role, narrative, diaries, letters and reports.

Contents	
Plot books	22
Flashbacks, flash-forward and dreams	25
Eyewitnesses	26
Writing in the frame	26

Drama strategies

Freeze-frames
Forum Theatre
Writing in role

Overview

Whilst freeze-frames are an excellent way to explore texts at a deeper level to support reading for meaning (See **DRAMA AND READING FOR MEANING AGES 4-11 by Larraine S. Harrison**), they can also be a useful way to support the teaching of writing. From planning a narrative to speculating about a story or writing in role, they can provide a context and a visual stimulus to motivate and feed the writing.

Plot books

These plot books originated from an idea by *Paul Johnson*, whose work has inspired many teachers and children to design, create and make their own books.

You can find other ideas for making different kinds of books in the following:

GET WRITING: CREATIVE BOOK-MAKING PROJECTS FOR CHILDREN AGES 4-7
GET WRITING: CREATIVE BOOK-MAKING PROJECTS FOR CHILDREN AGES 7-12

The basic outline of this work is the same for all ages, with simpler versions for key stage one. Freeze-frames are used here as visual prompts for making plot books. A class version, using freeze-frames with sentences to convey key elements of the plot, serves as a model before the children go on to compose their own plot books.

A plot book pares a story down to its bare bones and is designed to help pupils understand the difference between a plot and a story. The small size of the plot book in comparison to a storybook both indicates and necessitates the need for more brevity than a full narrative.

At key stage one, the plots are likely to follow a simple narrative structure of beginning, middle and end but at key stage two, they can focus on common story types such as the plot for a quest or a wishing tale. Children can use the plot books to experiment with different ways of organising a narrative such as a plot where the story opens with a problem, a bad deed or a villain or a flashback.

Planning and resources

You will need

- Space at the front of the class for a small group to make a freeze-frame;
- A blank plot book for each child and one for the demonstration. The books need to be around 8 × 7 cm with a 1-cm margin all around each page. They need to have a front and back with at least four pages inside. The margins help keep the writing central and also help children organise their thinking;
- A list of different types of prompts for the plot books is as follows:
  Front cover: *Title and author*
  Page 1: *Who is in the story, where are they and what is happening at the start?*
  Page 2: *Who or what else is in the story?*
  Page 3: *The Gamechanger: What changes make the story interesting?*
  Page 4: *How does the story end?*
  Back cover: *Blurb*

What to do

The drama

- (Optional) Some classes may need to apply the plot prompts to an existing text first, before attempting to create their own class story. If this is the case then choose a very simple story that children know well and produce a freeze-frame to illustrate the answer to each prompt along with a simple sentence.
- Explain that you will work together with the children to create a plot for a short story. Talk about the difference between a plot and a story.
- Talk about some possibilities for the plot. These could be related to the class topic or you can suggest an idea such as *Someone's pet goes missing* or *A character is afraid of something and gets teased until they conquer their fear*. The amount of support you provide will depend on the needs of the class but keep it as simple as possible.
- Once you have agreed on a rough plot, use the first prompt: *Who is in the story, where are they and what are they doing?*

- Ask a child or group of children to come to the front of the class to represent the character or characters they have suggested. Use an appropriate item of clothing or an object to signify the character for younger children and/or an adhesive name tag(s) for older children.
- Work with the class to produce a freeze-frame to represent the character(s) and setting at the start of the story. Use minimal props to represent the setting, as they can be time-consuming and prove to be a distraction.
- Ask the class what the character(s) is doing, where they are likely to be looking and what they are feeling at this moment, before making the freeze-frame to the words *1,2,3 Freeze ... 1,2,3 relax.*
- Then work with the class to create a suitable sentence to describe the freeze-frame in answer to the questions in the prompt e.g. *a boy sails a boat on a river; two children walk on a beach.*
- Make the freeze-frame again, but after the word *Freeze*, read out the sentence before saying *1,2,3 relax.*
- If appropriate to the story, repeat this process to make a second freeze-frame with a sentence to answer the next prompt: *bring someone or something else into the story* e.g. *the children see a shark in the water.*
- Repeat with the third prompt: *What interesting thing happens next?* Point out that this can be something unusual, naughty, scary, dangerous or funny e.g. *the shark has a tummy ache so the children give it some medicine.*
- Talk about how the story might end and decide on a sentence before making a final freeze-frame e.g. *the shark tries to eat the children but they escape.*
- Collect ideas for a suitable title and book cover design and a blurb for the back of the storybook. Use this as an opportunity to talk about these features as persuasive texts.
- Take one of the blank plot books and fill in the plot with the help of the children so they can see what the end result will look like.

The plot books

- Allow pairs of children time to brainstorm and record some ideas for their plot books based on the given prompts.
- Give each child a blank plot book and access to the prompts to make their plot book. They may want to write the plot in rough first before deciding on their plot. You may like to provide some suggestions for the gamechanger or interesting event such as the following:

Someone becomes scared
A stranger appears
A mysterious object is found
An accident happens
There is an argument
Someone tells a lie
Someone thinks they are being followed

Something dangerous happens
Something funny happens

- When children have completed the written parts of their plot books, ask them to provide a small illustration for the cover and decorate some or all of the margins with a design that is linked to the plot.
- Ask children to read out their plots. Then either as a class or as individuals, choose a plot and write part of it as a story to demonstrate the difference between the plot and the story.

> **Extension activity**
>
> The plot books can form a plot library where children can write a story based on someone else's plot or all the children can write the same plot to see how different they are. This can be a useful way to demonstrate how a plot is a guide that needs to be elaborated and can be interpreted in many ways.

Further suggestions

Key stage one: significant moments from stories or real events can be explored via freeze-frames and then presented as drawings with a written description. These can be displayed in various forms such as in zigzag books or the drawing presented centrally as if on a stage. Between 1 and 3 moments are usually sufficient.

Key stage two: small groups brainstorm ideas for stories and then each group presents the idea for their gamechanger/moment of change via a freeze-frame and caption before writing their stories individually.

Flashbacks, flash-forward and dreams

Freeze-frames can provide a useful way for children to explore, predict and then write about what happened before and/or after an existing story but they can also be a useful way to consider how and where to incorporate these features into their own story writing.

Dreams can also be expressed in a freeze-frame in preparation for writing. Models from reading are essential for children to appreciate the impact of these techniques.

VARJAK PAW by S.F. Said provides a good example of how dreams can be incorporated into the narrative structure, and **ANGEL'S CHILD by Larraine S. Harrison** begins with a poem about a legend in the past which has important implications for the storyline.

Key stage one: a freeze-frame reflecting one of the children's ideas about what could have or might happen before and/or after a well-known story can be created at the front of the class by a small group. This then provides the visual focus for subsequent writing.

Key stage two: children can work in groups to present a frozen depiction of what they think happened before or after a given moment from a story or text. They can also bring the freeze-frame to life for a minute to add improvised dialogue before freezing it again. This then forms the basis of their writing.

Eyewitnesses

When presenting a freeze-frame of a moment from a narrative with a group at the front of the class, it may be possible to find roles for the rest of the class who could then write diaries, witness statements, letters or reports about what they have seen e.g. the people at the fair who witnessed the moment the little girl refused to let Dave buy Dogger back in **DOGGER by Shirley Hughes** or the Danish warriors who were there when Beowulf announced he would save them from Grendel in **BEOWULF by Charles Keeping and Kevin Crossley Holland.**

You can also invent roles such as onlookers or passers-by. Key stage one children can take on the roles of creatures such as birds or other creatures who witnessed the event. If the freeze-frame is brought to life for a few seconds, key stage two children can take on the roles of detectives watching the freeze-frame as if on a security camera.

Characters in the actual freeze-frame could be given the option to write either as a participant writing a diary or letter about what happened to them at the moment of the freeze-frame or take on eyewitness roles like the rest of the class.

Writing in the frame

There are times when a piece of writing can be added to a freeze-frame. This could be a poster on a wall, a letter in someone's pocket, a page of a diary, a piece of information or a list, depending on the focus. Children can work in pairs to suggest the first few lines of the piece of writing and then complete it after the freeze-frame activity or the writing can be composed as a class. For example, as part of a freeze-frame about The Three Billy Goats Gruff, there may be a poster on the bridge warning people about the troll. This would include a description and what to do if the troll is seen, etc. If the freeze-frame is set in a house or building, there could be all kinds of writing around that children could complete and all kinds of written material can end up in a character's pocket or on the ground.

3 Strange hot-seating

Opportunities for writing

Non-chronological reports, information pages, descriptive writing, witness statements, diary entries and poems with personification.

Contents	
Real creatures	28
Imaginary creatures	30
Objects and the environment	33

Drama strategies

Hot-seating
Teacher-in-role

Overview

Hot-seating is where someone sits on a designated chair to be questioned in role by the class, who may or may not be in role themselves. Most teachers are familiar with hot-seating characters from stories to develop reading for meaning (See **DRAMA AND READING FOR MEANING AGES 4-11 by Larraine S. Harrison**) but non-human roles can provide a focus for different kinds of writing including information pages, witness statements, diary entries and poetry with personification.

There are various ways of organising hot-seating, so whether you take the hot-seat yourself or invite children to be hot-seated as individuals, pairs or groups, your choice will depend on the age and needs of the class and your writing objective. However, if you are using hot-seating to provide a model or information, the person in the hot-seat must be in a position to provide it. When a teacher takes the hot-seat as in many of the examples here, it provides an opportunity to model the content for the writing and an example of personification.

Real creatures

Hot-seating someone in role as a real creature, whether that be an animal, bird, reptile or insect can illicit sufficient information for children to write a page about the creature for an information book or website. It also provides an opportunity for children to devise appropriate questions to gain information for their writing. Books, like **INTERVIEW WITH A TIGER** and **INTERVIEW WITH A SHARK by Andy Seed,** provide excellent models of questions laced with a touch of humour.

KEY STAGE ONE EXAMPLE

Planning and resources

Select a suitable creature for children to write about as an information page.

You will need

- A designated chair for the hot-seat;
- A piece of material or other item to wear as a sign of role. This needs to be appropriate for your chosen creature such as a black scarf for a mole;
- Books and/or other resources to model questions about creatures and how the facts are presented on the page.

What to do

- Children may initially gain more information if the teacher plays the role of the creature. If you are taking up a non-human role like this, then make it clear that you will not try to look or sound like the creature, but will answer as if the creature could really talk. You can use a piece of material of an appropriate colour for the creature or some other small item as a sign of role to make it even clearer.
- Work with the children to devise appropriate questions beforehand and designate specific children to ask them, with the caveat that anyone can ask other questions if they think of them at the time. If children fail to cover all the main questions, it's best to introduce them yourself in role by saying something like *I expect you're wondering ...*
- Stop the hot-seating once the main questions have been answered, to ensure the children remain engaged.

'Publishing' the writing

- Ask children to create a page about the creature for an information book for their book corner or for a classroom display, including sketches and sentences about the creature. Children can create this work in pairs or as individuals or you can work with the children to compose this page as a class. Use models from real information books about similar creatures to guide their work.

- If possible find a real information page about this particular creature and invite children to check they have covered everything in their work.

> **Extension activity**
>
> Groups or pairs of confident children can research facts about different creatures and then be hot-seated by the rest of the class. They can use the same questions each time to produce either a question-and-answer book or an information page.

KEY STAGE TWO EXAMPLE

Planning and resources

You will need

- A designated chair for the hot-seat;
- Books and/or resources as models for the writing.

What to do

- Organise the children into small groups and allocate each group a specific creature. You may want to choose creatures from a similar group such as those with claws, or creatures who live in the same geographical area or you can choose creatures from a range of different habitats.
- Work with the class to talk about the kinds of questions you might want answering from an information book about different creatures and make a list of the most likely ones that definitely need answering. Refer to any books with questions and answers about creatures and use these as models.
- Ask the class to research answers to these questions about their creature, ready to be hot-seated by the class. Ask them to think of any other questions that may not be on the main list.
- Groups are then hot-seated in role as their creatures. Decide beforehand who will ask which questions from the class, but make it clear that others can ask other questions too. Chair the hot-seating to ensure everyone in the group playing the creatures has an opportunity to respond if they wish.

'Publishing' the writing

- Ask children to write an information page about their creature and combine them into one book for the class book corner or as a webpage or blog. Alternatively, children can pitch their work as a book for younger children to go in the book corner of a key stage one class.

Extension activity

- Children write an imaginary diary of a day in the life of their creature.
- Children read poems written in or including creature's voices e.g. **DISAPPOINTED FROG** (from **RIDING A LION**) by Coral Rumble and **BETWEEN THE DOG AND THE WOLF** (from **WEIRD WILD AND WONDERFUL**) by James Carter and then write their own.

Imaginary creatures

Hot-seating imaginary creatures can be carried out in much the same way as with real creatures with the aim of writing an information page, but if children create their own creatures there are ways to introduce the hot-seating that also provide opportunities for descriptive writing and writing poetry and news reports.

KEY STAGE ONE EXAMPLE: CREATING A MONSTER

Planning and resources

You will need

- A cleared space large enough for all the children to stand in a circle or similar shape. Where space is limited, children can sit together in the story corner;
- A few books or resources with pictures of different kinds of monsters e.g. **WHERE THE WILD THINGS ARE** by Maurice Sendak;
- A plain dark scarf or cloak as a sign of teacher-in-role;
- A designated chair or cushion for the hot-seat.

What to do

- Ask the children what they think of when someone says the word *Monster*. Explain that you will be helping them create their very own class monster. Refer to the pictures of monsters you have with you and talk about the variations, favourites, most scary, etc.
- Work with the children to talk about and make a list of what their monster might look like and how it might behave. Mention that their monster might be a creature that changes how it looks now and again.
- Ask the children to stand in the space as if they were standing around their sleeping monster. Talk about its shape and where its head might be, etc. If you are using the story corner instead of a space, ask the children to move back slightly to create a small space and imagine the monster is asleep in front of them.
- Explain that in a few minutes you will ask the children, either individually or in pairs, to tell everyone what the monster looks like from where they are standing or sitting. Give

them time to think of just one thing to describe the monster and start with the words *I can see …* You may need to provide some examples for less confident or younger children such as *I can see two spiky horns.* Encourage children to add adjectives if appropriate. Older or more confident writers can write this as a sentence on a small whiteboard.

- When children have decided what they can see, walk around the outside shape of the monster and point to each child or pair to speak out their observations or point to them if they are sitting. It may be useful to repeat each contribution to make sure everyone can hear and add status.
- Ask the children to think about what the monster might be like, what it eats, where it lives, does it have any family or friends, does it have a name, is it scared of anything?, etc.
- Explain that they will be writing an information page later on, to tell everyone about their monster.
- Suggest that they hot-seat the monster to find out the answers to these questions for their writing. Draw an imaginary safety screen in the air in front of the monster to reassure the children that they will be safe.
- Ask the children if they can pretend that you are the voice of the monster when you put on the scarf and sit on a chair in the middle of the space where the monster is sleeping. Make it clear that you will not talk in a very different voice but you will be talking as if you are the monster. Talk about what kind of questions they need to ask the monster and ask for a volunteer to ask the first question or the first few questions.
- Put on the scarf to take on the role of the voice of the monster and start the hot-seating with the word *Action*. It's important not to use a strange voice or come across as scary as this can make it difficult for children to interact with you. Try to be a sympathetic character with feelings. As far as possible use some of the children's previous speculations about what the monster might be like when answering the questions. If children forget to ask a particular question then add it yourself by saying *I expect you are wondering…* When you feel children have enough information stop the drama using the word *Freeze*, take off the scarf and move off the chair.
- Ask the children what they found out about the monster from the hot-seating. This may sound obvious to an adult, but young children take the pretence seriously and if you ask this with confidence they will often respond as if you didn't know.

'Publishing' the writing

- Use the hot-seating information to work with the class to write an information page for the book corner display or for others in the school.

Extension activity

Children create a story about their monster, either as a class or as individuals.

KEY STAGE TWO EXAMPLE: THE DISCOVERY

Planning and resources

You will need

- Copies of books with imaginary creatures such as **THE LAND OF NEVERBELIEVE by Norman Messenger** or nonsense poems like **THE JUMBLIES by Edward Lear**;
- A scarf or other item as a sign of teacher-in-role as a journalist;
- A designated chair for the hot-seat.

What to do

- Ask the children to imagine the following scenario:

    An explorer has sent a message to the media revealing an exciting discovery. They have found a previously undiscovered small island that appears to be inhabited by some very strange creatures that have never been seen before. They have yet to explore the island in more depth but will give one interview via a video call on what they have found so far.

- Ask the children to talk in pairs to speculate on what these creatures might be like and then bring everyone back to share ideas.
- Ask the children to accept that you will play the part of the explorer and ask them to play the parts of the media at the first interview. Talk about what questions the media might ask in order to obtain a good newsworthy story and list a few for them to refer to. Explain that this is the kind of hot-seating where everyone is in role.
- Use the words *Action* and *Freeze* to start and stop the hot-seating. Choose one child to ask the first question but make it clear that anyone can ask a question after that. Remind them that this is meant to be online and agree how the media journalists will indicate they have a question e.g. by raising a hand as on a zoom call.
- Place a chair in front of the group for the explorer and then put on the scarf to take on the role of the explorer. Try not to speak in a very different voice as this can be a distraction but the tone will be that of an excited explorer talking to the media. Use the previous speculation ideas from the class to tell the media what you have seen so far but make it clear that you have seen evidence that there are many more creatures yet to find. As soon as you feel the questions have dried up, tell them you have to leave but will meet them again soon. Then stop the hot-seating on the word *Freeze*, as you leave the chair and take off the scarf.
- Ask the children to summarise what they have discovered and think about what headline or tagline the media might use.
- Working on their own or in pairs, ask the children to create their own strange creature that was discovered on the island. Make it clear that this can be as strange as they like. Refer to the books for examples of strange creatures or beings.

'Publishing' the writing

- Once children have created their creatures, ask them to create a page about their creature for the information book written by the explorer when he/she returned home.

Collect all the pages into a book for the book corner. Agree on a suitable title and add the explorer's name as the author.

Extension activities

- Children write an entry in the explorer's diary describing the day their creature was discovered.
- Children write the media report about the first and/or the final interview with the explorer.
- Children write a poem based on their creature, using relevant poems as models.

Objects and the environment

Objects and features of the environment, such as plants, a wood, a river or a mountain, can be personified in the hot-seat to enable them to speak about their experiences as eyewitnesses with perspectives on events. The objects often relate to events in novels or well-known stories such as the bridge crossed by The Three Billy Goats Gruff or the imagination box in **THE IMAGINATION BOX by Martyn Ford**. Environmental features, such as a tree or a river, may be part of the setting of a story, but they can also be geographical features that have a view on environmental issues such as pollution. Hot-seating in this way provides an opportunity for children to use personification when writing eyewitness accounts or points of view. Personification also lends itself well to writing poetry, with many examples to use as models.

KEY STAGE ONE EXAMPLE

Key stage one, children often find it easier to hot-seat objects that resemble the human form such as toys or objects linked to traditional stories. If a teacher-in-role as an object is in the hot-seat, the object can express confusion about what it has witnessed, thus creating the need for younger children to explain.

Planning and resources

Choose a familiar story and an object that would have witnessed the main events.

You will need

- A designated chair for the hot-seat;
- A scarf as a sign of teacher-in-role;
- Examples of personification of objects in stories and rhymes such as **THE DAY THE CRAYONS QUIT by Drew Daywalk** and Hey Diddle Diddle.

What to do

- Talk about your examples of personified objects.
- Identify the story and the object you have chosen. Talk about where it is placed in connection to the story and what it might tell us if it could talk e.g.

    On the wall In Red Riding Hood's grandma's bedroom there was a mirror. It was there when the wolf came to the door. If it could speak, I wonder what it would tell us about what it saw that day.

    If Jack's beanstalk could talk, I wonder what it would say about what happened in the story.

- Ask the children to pretend that the object could talk. Then ask them if you can pretend to be the voice of the object when you sit on the hot-seat, so they can ask it some questions. Show them the scarf you will wear so they are clear when you are in the role. Talk about what questions they might ask. Include questions about how the object felt and what they may have been thinking at various points in the story e.g.
    - **Mirror:** How did you feel when you saw the wolf coming into Grandma's bedroom? What did you think might happen?
    - **Beanstalk:** How did you feel when Jack's mum threw you away in the garden when you were just a little bean? How did you feel when Jack chopped you down? Do you know why he did it?
    - **Bridge:** Do you like having a troll living underneath you? Were you surprised when the troll didn't eat the first Billy Goat when he trip-trapped across you? Do you know why?
- Create a list of a few questions and allocate a child to ask each one. These questions are likely to be based on what the object saw and how they felt or what they were thinking at various points in the narrative. This can be a challenging concept for younger children to grasp, so if this is the case it may be best to limit the number of questions.
- Sit in the hot-seat with your sign of role. Use the words *Action* and *Freeze* to start and stop the drama. Tell the children who you are and ask them if they have any questions. If children hesitate or there are any other problems, you can come out of the role to help out or make suggestions and then return to the hot-seat. This is likely to be very short but when the key questions have been answered it is best to stop the drama rather than trying to fill in the time with extra details that may confuse the children.
- Ask the children what they have found out from the hot-seat. Then work with them to produce a piece of writing written in the first person about what the object saw and felt e.g. *I am Jack's beanstalk. I was upset when his mum didn't want me...*
- Whether this is organised as one piece of writing as a whole class or as individual pieces of writing will depend on the confidence of the children.
- Add the completed writing to a wall display based on the story, along with an illustration of the object.

Extension activity

Invite confident children to sit in the hot-seat in the role of another object from the same or a different story to answer questions about what they saw and felt. Then invite all the children to draw the object and write a couple of sentences about it in the first person.

Strange hot-seating 35

KEY STAGE TWO EXAMPLE

At key stage two, children often enjoy the challenge of devising questions to hot-seat an object and/or be hot-seated themselves in this kind of role. The hot-seating can also lead to a character study about the owner of the object based on the information from the hot-seating. Hot-seating an object works best when linked to a story where the same setting hosts a significant amount of action such as the lighthouse accommodation in **FEATHERLIGHT by Peter Bunzl** or the kitchen in Ynysfach in **WHEN THE WAR CAME HOME by Lesley Parr.**

Stories with an environmental setting can tell parts of the story from that perspective e.g. what Bear Island thought about the events there in **THE LAST BEAR by Hannah Gold** or what the river Thames thought about the activities of the Junior Mudlarks in **OCTOBER, OCTOBER by Katya Balen**.

Plannng and resources

- Choose an object or environmental feature from a well-known story that you can represent in the first hot-seat. Then plan what you saw and how you might feel about it.
- Choose objects or features from another story for children to write about using personification.

You will need

- *Examples of personification of objects e.g.* **THE DAY THE CRAYONS QUIT** by Drew Daywalt;
- *A designated chair for your hot-seating;*
- *Extension Activity – poems illustrating personification of non-human objects or features e.g.* **WHO SHE'S MEANT TO BE** (from **RIDING A LION**) by Coral Rumble.

What to do

- Ask the children to imagine that your chosen object or environmental feature had a voice and an opinion and link this to personification. Use your examples as models.
- Ask the children to imagine you could be the voice of this object/feature when sitting on the hot-seat. Talk about and list the kinds of questions they may want to ask you in this role, including what you witnessed and your opinion of the various events. Allocate one child to ask you the first question.
- Using the words *Action* and *Freeze* to start and stop the drama, sit on the chair and begin the hot-seating in role as your object or feature.
- Ask the children to summarise what they have discovered from the hot-seating and work with the class to write it as a witness statement or a diary entry in the first person. Alternatively, this can be written as a monologue or dialogue with someone asking questions as in a hot-seating activity.
- Ask pairs of children to select one of the objects or features from another story or a different part of the same story and talk about what it witnessed, using your hot-seating responses as a guide.

- Ask individual children or pairs to write about the object in the first person as a witness statement or a diary entry.

> **Extension activity**
>
> Invite children to read and write poems that use personification of non-humans e.g. ***THE MOON SPEAKS*** and ***THE ELEPHANT'S ODE TO THE DUNG BEETLE*** (from ***WEIRD WILD AND WONDERFUL***) **by James Carter.**

4 Viewpoints

Opportunities for writing

Writing a balanced argument, an opinion, letters and lists and news reports in role.

Contents	
Balanced arguments and opinions	37
Cats versus dogs	38
Views on zoos	39
The discussion book	43
Character viewpoints: Diaries, letters and postcards	45

Drama strategies

Conscience alley
Freeze-frames
Mantle of the expert
Teacher or puppet-in-role
Where do you stand?

Balanced arguments and opinions

KEY STAGE ONE OVERVIEW: VERBAL DEBATES AND WRITTEN OPINIONS

Whilst children in key stage one would not be expected to write a balanced argument, it may be useful to introduce them to the idea of opposing arguments via stories and verbal debates. This can lead to non-chronological writing such as letters based on their own opinions. Teacher-in-role or puppet-in-role, for example, can present the children with an opportunity to consider opposing arguments about a particular issue. After considering both sides of the argument and discussing the issue, children form their own opinions, which they then communicate to the character via letter writing.

DOI: 10.4324/9781003315742-6

KEY STAGE ONE EXAMPLE: CATS VERSUS DOGS

In this example, a puppet needs help about whether to have a cat or a dog as a pet. The children weigh up the arguments and then formulate their own opinions which they send to the puppet via a letter.

Links to reading

CATS VERSUS DOGS by Elizabeth Carney
WOULD YOU RATHER: SHAKE LIKE A DOG OR CLIMB LIKE A CAT? by Camilla de la Bedoyere

Planning and resources

You will need

- A puppet in a bed such as a shoe box;
- A sign saying CAT with a picture of a cat on it;
- A sign saying DOG with a picture of a dog on it;
- A note from the puppet thanking the children for their help.

What to do

- Introduce the puppet who communicates by whispering to you. It is looking unhappy. Ask the puppet why it seems to be unhappy. Tell the children that the puppet is worried because it wants a pet but can't decide whether to have a dog or a cat. It only has room for one pet in its small house, but it does have a garden. It asks the children to help it decide.
- Ask the children if any of them have cats or dogs as pets and how they feel about them. Try to bring out all the children's opinions about whether a cat makes a better pet than a dog. Add other arguments if necessary.
- The puppet tells the children that it is very tired after not sleeping due to thinking about the problem. It needs to go to sleep and then think about all the arguments, but is worried it won't remember what everyone said. Offer to write the arguments down for the puppet so it can read them later. Then put the puppet to sleep in the box.
- Ask the children to remind you as you write the arguments down in two lists opposite each other.
- Use the **Where Do You Stand?** drama strategy in the following way: put the sign and image saying CAT on one side of the room and the sign and image saying DOG on the other. Give the children a few minutes to think about what their advice would be to the puppet about having a cat or a dog as a pet and then ask them to stand on the side of the room with the sign that indicates their choice. If they are still unsure they should stand in the middle of the room, between the two signs. Once they have made their choices ask a few children why they have made that choice, including those that are undecided.

Audience and purpose

- Suggest they write a letter to the puppet, giving their advice and opinions after hearing all the arguments. These can be written by individuals giving their own opinions or as a whole class summarising their different views.
- Finally, bring the puppet back to look at the list of arguments and receive their letter(s) to take away and read. Then put the puppet back in the box.
- Sometime later, send the children a letter from the puppet thanking them for their advice. The puppet's final decision will depend on what you think would be the most acceptable to the children.

Further suggestions

- Use the **Where Do You Stand?** drama strategy to stimulate talking and writing about amusing choices, such as those in the **WOULD YOU RATHER?** books **by Camilla de la Bedoyere** about sharks, dinosaurs and dung beetles.
- Write a letter to the children from a character facing a dilemma in a class story e.g. Mrs Lambchop in **FLAT STANLEY IN SPACE by Jeff Brown** wants to know whether Stanley and the family should go on the space mission. Talk with the children about the opposing arguments before asking them to reply with written advice.

KEY STAGE TWO OVERVIEW

Conscience alley is the best-known drama strategy for presenting a visual representation of a balanced argument. In this activity, opposing points of view are physically represented and separated by children forming two lines opposite each other to make an alley. The two lines represent two different arguments. A character or a person undecided about the outcomes of the issue then walks down the alley to listen to the opposing arguments before making a choice.

Other drama strategies such as freeze-frames indicating biased viewpoints and writing balanced arguments in the role of journalists can also be useful.

KEY STAGE TWO EXAMPLE 1: VIEWS ON ZOOS

Links to reading

THE LAST TIGER by Petr Horacek
BEHIND THE SCENES AT THE ZOO by D.K.
ZOO by Anthony Browne

Planning and resources

You will need

- (Optional) Collect visual prompts and/or other resources on zoos for children who have limited knowledge and experience of zoos;

- Make a sign saying **FOR ZOOS** and a sign saying **AGAINST ZOOS**;
- Make a list of arguments for and against zoos, written as short statements. Use the following as a guide and/or plan to work with the children to complete the list:

  Six arguments in favour of zoos
  1. Zoos can educate people about wild animals
  2. Zoos keep wild animals safe from being attacked
  3. Zoos can save rare animals from becoming extinct
  4. Many people would never see wild animals if it wasn't for zoos
  5. Zoos are popular and provide jobs for people
  6. Zoos can give wild animals a better quality of life than in the wild

  Six arguments against zoos
  1. People can learn more about wild animals from books and online than zoos
  2. Most animals have natural ways to keep safe and don't need zoos
  3. It's better to protect rare animals in their natural habitat than zoos
  4. Films of animals in the wild give a better idea of what they're like than zoos
  5. Zoos are expensive to run. There are better ways to provide jobs
  6. Zoos cause animals to become stressed (Zoochosis) and are unnatural and degrading

- If you are using a ready-made list as a guide, make a copy of the list to share with the children, then write each of the statements on separate strips of paper. Children need one statement strip between two, so in large classes, you may need to make extra copies. In smaller classes, the slips can be given to individual children instead of pairs and/or you can combine similar arguments to reduce the number of slips. Include a few blank strips of paper or small whiteboards for any additional arguments suggested by the children;
- If you plan to compose the list of arguments with the children you will need small whiteboards or blank slips of paper, one for each argument.

What to do

- Ask the children what they think of when they hear the word *Zoo*. Ask whether anyone has visited a zoo and what they think about them. Use visual prompts if necessary. Talk about the difference between a zoo, a safari park and an animal sanctuary.
- Invite children's initial thoughts on the question *Do we still need zoos?* Collect arguments for and against zoos and then share your pre-prepared list, adding any ideas from the children if appropriate. If you are using the children's list of arguments, then record them as short statements for everyone to see and record each one on a small whiteboard or slip of paper.
- Explain to the children that the forthcoming drama work will help them write a balanced argument about zoos. Make it clear that they will be expected to consider and write about each argument fairly, but will eventually be invited to express their own opinions.
- Organise the class into pairs and give each pair a whiteboard or slip of paper with one argument on it.
- Place the sign saying FOR ZOOS on one side of the room and the sign saying AGAINST ZOOS on the other. Then ask the pairs to decide whether the argument on their paper is for or against zoos and ask them to stand on the appropriate side of the room.

Viewpoints   41

- Ask a child on one side to read out their argument and then ask the other side if anyone has a counterargument for that particular point, to balance it out. Carry on with this until all the arguments have been covered.
- Display the list of arguments so the children can refer to it when necessary.

Conscience alley

- Using their given arguments, ask the children to form an alleyway of two lines representing for and against zoos. Ask them to organise themselves so each argument is directly opposite its counterargument in the lines if possible.
- Walk down the centre of the alleyway to hear each argument and counterargument in turn as you pass by the children. Point to the children to indicate when it's their turn if necessary.

Bias versus balance

- Ask the children to imagine that a new zoo was opening in the imaginary seaside town of Sabden (or another fictitious place name) and that news reporters and photographers were invited to the opening ceremony. Explain that there are three online newspapers in the town that all have different views about zoos: The Sabden Weekly, The Sabden Express and The Sabden Independent.
    Explain the following:
    The Sabden Weekly loves the idea of a new zoo. They asked their photographer to take a photo showing what a great thing the zoo was for the town and how everyone supports it, even though some do not.
- Ask the children to think about how they could make a whole class freeze-frame of this photo, as if they were the people at the opening of the zoo. If space is limited, ask a small group to make the freeze-frame at the front of the class. Discuss what kind of photo would convey a positive message about zoos, such as people smiling at the animals or feeding them, etc.
- Allow some time in pairs for children to decide where they were standing and what they were doing the moment the photo was taken. Ask them to freeze into this position when you take the imaginary photo using the words *This is the photo taken by the Sabden Weekly on the day the new zoo opened ...1,2,3, Freeze... 1.2.3. relax.*
- Talk about what the headline might be and add a caption that supports their positive views. Then repeat the freeze-frame by reading out the heading and caption, followed by *1.2.3...relax.*
- Now introduce the next online newspaper called The Sabden Express. The journalists in this organisation are against zoos. They feel strongly that zoos are not a good idea. Ask the children to create a freeze-frame of the photo that they took. How might it be different from the one taken by The Sabden Weekly? Would they select different things to focus on? Would they include the people smiling at the animals, etc.? Repeat the freeze-frame in the same way as with the Sabden Weekly, adding different headlines and a caption to reflect their different views.

- Ask the children to take on the roles of the journalists in the third online newspaper called The Sabden Independent. They try to present a balanced view of things before stating their own opinions. Talk about what their photo might focus on and what their headline and caption might be to reflect a balanced view?
- Working in pairs or individually, ask children to produce a rough sketch of The Sabden Independent's photo with a headline above and a caption below. Then share the headlines and captions for discussion.

Audience and purpose: Taking notes and writing in role

- Ask each of the children to take on the role of a journalist working for The Sabden Independent. They are to attend a debate about zoos at the town hall and write it up as a news report afterwards.
- Organise an imaginary debate in Sabden Town Hall between two individual characters from the town to represent both sides of the argument. You can use teacher-in-role to play one of the parts and ask another adult or a confident child to play the opposing part or ask two confident children to play the roles. Whatever you choose, ask the class beforehand what arguments each character should use first as their main point and invite them to offer any other advice on how the arguments should be presented. Children also enjoy making up the characters if appropriate. The characters speak one at a time. The children attend the debate in role as journalists/reporters from The Sabden Independent, making notes as they listen. They are invited to ask questions of each character after the presentations and then write up their reports after the debate. It may be worth reminding children that, in reality, there would only be one report on this debate in The Sabden Independent.
- Use either of these versions as an opportunity to teach or remind children of the features of a balanced argument, such as the need for examples or evidence to back up some of the points and the use of adverbials and causal/contrasting conjunctions. Talk about how to write an appropriate introduction to the issues that will precede their account of the balanced arguments. Ask children to consider their own views about zoos after listening to both sides of the argument. Use this to introduce the idea of a final conclusive paragraph for the article which will include their own view written in the first person.

Extension activities

- Design and produce an information leaflet or online page for children, providing a summary of the arguments about zoos. Children need to tailor their arguments to meet the needs of the intended audience.
- Look at webpages of zoos to learn about their history and their perspectives on the arguments e.g. **London and Whipsnade Zoo** at www.zsl.org.
- Research famous zoo animals of the past, such as Brumas, the first polar bear, born in London Zoo in 1949 or Guy the Gorilla, and discuss the different viewpoints people may have now about their treatment and their lives compared to the past.

Writers' reflections

- Introduce or remind the children of the meaning of the word *biased*. Talk about the biased reporting of The Sabden Weekly and The Sabden Express and ask the children to consider if and when this can happen in the real world of news reporting.
- Ask the children to reflect on how difficult they found it to write about an argument they didn't agree with. Talk about how news reporters sometimes use positive vocabulary in their written articles to make their viewpoint seem more attractive or vice versa to undermine an opposite point of view.

Further suggestions

Link the arguments to topic work or social issues e.g.

- Worms are disappearing from our gardens. Is this good or bad?
- Should wolves be introduced back into the UK?
- Should dogs be banned from parks?
- Should cars be banned from all towns?
- Is it good to be famous?
- Should children be limited to one hour a day online?

KEY STAGE TWO EXAMPLE 2: THE DISCUSSION BOOK

Children often produce their best discursive writing when they are interested in and/or have prior knowledge about the topic they are discussing. Having confidence in the content allows them to focus more on the features and quality of the writing. This activity provides an opportunity for children to select and write a discursive text on a topic of their choice but within an imaginary context.

Whilst it's possible to carry out the activity without using a dramatic context, the creation of imaginary characters adds to the fun which can increase children's engagement and motivation to write.

What to do

Setting the imaginary context

- Invite the children to take on the role of a group of experts who are hoping to contribute to a new book entitled *The Discussion Book*. The book is aimed at children and teachers looking for interesting topics to debate in school.
- Explain that to prepare for this role, each child will need to decide on a topic they could be an expert in. It needs to be an area they already have an interest in and/or know something about. Their area of expertise can be anything that appeals to and is suitable for children, but it must involve a discussion question.
- Explain that the Contents page of *The Discussion Book* will contain the names of the experts alongside a list of discussion questions that will appeal to children. Children will be asked to make up a suitable name for their expert with possibly a title such as a

professor or a doctor or some relevant qualifications. This is an opportunity to help children understand what people's titles and qualifications refer to. This will be followed by a 'Meet the Experts' page. Children will be asked to create the information for this page by providing a sketch of their expert and a short CV of their background.
- The body of the book will be the articles written by the experts about their discussion questions. These will contain arguments for and against, followed by the expert's own views.
- In preparation, allow some time for children to decide on their roles and their discussion questions. They should make a list of things they are interested in and a list of things they know a lot about. Encourage them to take their time to consider each option rather than choosing the first idea. They need to choose an area with potential for a discussion question. The choice is up to the child, but you might suggest they choose an area they feel confident to write about and have some background knowledge. Let children work in pairs for support and provide some suggestions as models. These can be areas of personal interest such as football teams, magical creatures, superheroes, dinosaurs, horses, video games, etc., or represent more global issues such as animals in danger of extinction, sea pollution, etc.
- Once children have chosen their area of interest, ask children to devise their discussion questions. Provide some examples e.g. Is football better than cricket? Is it right to use animals for entertainment? Are video games bad for children? Are comics better than books?
- When the discussion questions have been decided, ask the children to create their characters for the book and write their sections for the 'Meet the Experts' page.

(Optional Meet and Greet)

- Working in pairs, ask children to walk around the room on a given signal to meet other pairs. They should talk to each other in role as their experts. They should share their names, areas of expertise and discussion questions. After a short time, roughly after each pair has had an opportunity to share with two other pairs, stop the Meet and Greet and invite children to see how many discussion questions they could recall, along with any other details about the experts.
- If possible, type out the Contents page for the book, to add status.
- When children have written their balanced arguments and conclusions, invite the class to help compose a blurb for the back of the book and a suitable design for the cover. Then put everything together in a book entitled *The Discussion Book* and add it to the class book corner or school library.

Extension activity

Invite the class to vote to select one of the discussion questions in the book to discuss as a class, with the experts on hand to supply information. After the children have heard both sides of the argument, organise a Where Do You Stand? activity where children stand on a particular side of the room, according to which argument they prefer. Children who are undecided can stand in the middle. Choose a few children to verbally explain the reasons for their choices and/or ask all the children to record their reasons in writing.

Character viewpoints: Diaries, letters and postcards

Character viewpoints can relate to fictional or real-life incidents where different people might have different perspectives on the same event. Character or job references from different people in stories, showing how they feel about them or different perspectives on PSHE topics can be useful sources. Freeze-frames depicting key incidents can offer a visual depiction where children can discuss the different viewpoints prior to writing one viewpoint in role. This can be in the form of a diary, postcard or letter. Different children can write in role as different characters so their perspectives can be compared.

5 Bubbles, comics and playscripts

Opportunities for writing

Writing dialogue in speech bubbles, comic/graphic novel formats and playscripts and summaries of main points.

Contents	
An extra frame	46
The one-minute playscript (key stage two)	53
Silent movie scripts	58

Drama strategies

Freeze-frames
Improvisation
Performing playscripts

An extra frame

Creating an extra freeze-frame of a story or an event and adding speech bubbles that come to life is a useful way to demonstrate that speech bubbles are what the characters actually say. It also creates an opportunity for children to explore and imitate how writers of picture books, comics and graphic novels use images rather than words like *said* to indicate who is speaking. Some children can then go on to convert simple prose dialogue into speech bubbles and explore how to express direct speech, thoughts and sounds in comic/graphic novel format.

KEY STAGE ONE EXAMPLE: THE WATCHERS

Links to reading

Books with speech bubbles e.g.

LIZZIE AND THE BIRDS by Dawn and Mick Robertson
THE BIG BAD MOLE'S COMING by Martin Waddell

DOI: 10.4324/9781003315742-7

DON'T FORGET THE BACON by Pat Hutchins
SEND FOR A SUPERHERO by Michael Rosen

Books with direct speech in prose e.g.

SHHH QUIET by Nicola Kinnear
NO MATTER WHAT by Debi Gliori

Books in graphic novel format and illustrated fiction e.g.

NARWHAL UNICORN OF THE SEA by Ben Clanton
BUMBLE AND SNUG AND THE ANGRY PIRATES by Mark Bradley
GOOD ROSIE by Kate Di Camillo
ICED OUT by C. K. Smouha

Planning and resources

- Select a key moment from a familiar story with potential eyewitnesses e.g. birds looking through the window of the Three Bears' cottage when Goldilocks breaks Baby Bear's chair; forest creatures watching the wolf leave Red Riding Hood for Grandma's house; neighbours watching the family set off for a bear hunt; etc.
- (Extension Activity) Choose a familiar book and select an illustration of a key moment that includes a simple piece of dialogue written in prose. Make a large copy to share with the class. For example, the moment in **SHHH QUIET by Nicola Kinnear** when the four noisy animal friends hide from a bear. In this example, Fox, Squirrel, Racoon and Owl all make a simple comment or a sound that is expressed in prose. Another example is the moment in **NO MATTER WHAT by Debi Gliori** when Small is sitting with Large worrying that no one will love him because he is grumpy.

You will need

- At least one story or part of a story told in speech bubbles;
- Space at the front of the class for a small group to make a freeze-frame;
- Simple items to signify each character in the freeze-frame e.g. scarf, bag and masks;
- A large A4-sized speech bubble;
- Individual whiteboards;
- (Extension Activity) Examples of books written in a simple comic or graphic novel format.

What to do

Introduction and examples

- Draw children's attention to the idea of telling a story through speech bubbles by reading them at least one book as a model and talking about the effect.
- Suggest they could use speech bubbles in some of their own writing.

48 *Drama as a Helping Hand*

- Remind the children of another story that is not told in speech bubbles. Suggest you add speech bubbles to a key moment from that story to see what it might be like or which version they may prefer.

The drama

- Invite a group of children who are comfortable with performing to come to the front. With help from the class, ask the children to stand like the characters in that key moment to make a frozen picture called a freeze-frame. Give the children the items to symbolise their characters if appropriate. Ask them to freeze when you say the word *Freeze* and hold the freeze until you say *1,2,3, relax*.
- Ask the children which character would speak first if the freeze-frame came to life. Hold a speech bubble outline over the head of that character and ask the children in the class what might be written inside it. Then repeat with the other characters in turn.
- Tell the children that you would like to see what it would be like if the characters really did come to life and begin to speak. Make it clear that the characters might not say exactly what was suggested in the speech bubbles, but they might say something similar.
- Make the freeze-frame again. Ask the characters to come alive and speak to each other when you say the word *Action* and stop when you say the words *1,2,3, relax*. Give the children in the freeze-frame a minute to think of what they might say before you say *Action* and remind them who will speak first.
- The resulting dialogue is likely to be short and simple, especially with younger children, but if the characters have problems with the dialogue or you feel they could potentially say more, then freeze the action and ask for suggestions from the class or allow other children to have a turn at playing the characters.
- Ask the children to imagine they were creatures or people who saw what happened in the freeze-frame i.e. watchers/eyewitnesses. Specify who the 'watchers' were or invite the children to make suggestions.
- Suggest they prepare to make the freeze-frame again, but this time they should include all the 'watchers' and their speech bubbles.
- Invite children to speculate about what the 'watchers' might have felt about what they saw and what they might say in a speech bubble. If appropriate, refer to books where 'watchers' make comments such as the seagulls in **THE LIGHTHOUSE KEEPERS LUNCH by Ronda and David Armitage** and the birds in **LIZZIE AND THE BIRDS by Dawn Robertson**.

Teacher modelling

- Draw a large speech bubble on a whiteboard. Think aloud as you draft and edit an appropriate comment made by a 'watcher' and then write it clearly in your speech bubble. You may want to draft it somewhere else before adding it to the speech bubble. Whether you write the comment as a full sentence or a phrase will depend on the context and the learning objective.
- Then invite each child or pair to draw a large speech bubble on their whiteboards. Ask them to draft and edit a 'watchers' comment on paper first, then write their final version inside their speech bubble. Older or more confident children might be asked to write

their comments as a question or an exclamation. Encourage children to write clearly so their speech bubble can be read aloud during the freeze-frame.

Planning the performance

- Explain that the children who played the characters in the original freeze-frame will play those parts again in the whole class version. Since these children cannot also be 'watchers,' ask other children to hold up these 'watchers' speech bubbles during the freeze-frame or prop them up somewhere in the room so that everyone can read them.
- Children playing the 'watchers' can remain in the classroom area to make the freeze-frame, either standing or seated as appropriate.
- Invite children to indicate with a thumbs up during the freeze-frame if they want to read out their own speech bubble when you point to them. Otherwise, explain that you will read out the bubbles on their behalf. However, if you have a large class with limited concentration levels, it may be preferable to ask for one or two volunteers to read out their speech bubble and/or summarise or present an overview of the others.

The performance

- Using the same commands as in the first freeze-frame, make the whole class freeze-frame with the original characters and the 'watchers' holding up their speech bubbles. Read out and/or summarise the speech bubbles as previously planned.

Writers' reflections

- Ask the children why they have not written the words *he/she/they said* in the bubbles. Use this conversation to talk about how the image or picture tells readers who said the words, so there is no need to write the word *said*. If appropriate, refer to books to compare direct speech in speech bubbles to how it is written in prose. Some books, such as **LIZZIE AND THE BIRDS by Dawn Robertson,** have examples of direct speech in both prose and bubbles which are sometimes presented on the same page.
- Ask children if they enjoy reading books with speech bubbles and if so why.
- Ask children if they enjoy writing with speech bubbles and if so why.
- Invite older children to consider how they read books with speech bubbles e.g.
    Do you look at the pictures first or the speech bubbles first or both at the same time? If more than one character is speaking, how do you know who is speaking first?

Extension activities

Writing with speech bubbles

Invite children to use speech bubbles in their own writing as appropriate. For example, they could write part of an existing story or write part of their own story using drawings of characters with speech bubbles. Those who need more support could be given a writing frame with bubbles to fill in based on an illustration of a well-known story.

Converting prose to speech bubbles

Select an illustration from a familiar storybook that is accompanied by simple dialogue written in prose. For example, the illustration in **SHHH QUIET by Nicola Kinear** of the moment when the animals hide in a tree trunk after hearing a scary noise. Ask the children to identify the words spoken by each character in the prose and write these down inside bubble shapes on whiteboards.

Make a freeze-frame of this moment using a group at the front as before, but ask another group of children to stand behind each character to hold up the speech bubbles, so everyone can read them. Invite the class to read the bubbles with you one at a time as you point to each character, or read them yourself. Use this as an opportunity to reinforce the difference between writing direct speech in prose and in bubbles.

Exploring moments of decision

Ask a group of children to make a freeze-frame of a moment of decision in a story, such as the moment in **FARMER DUCK by Martin Waddell** where all the animals make a plan to evict the lazy farmer. Children then speculate about what might be in the characters' speech bubbles and write them out to share with the class. Use similar incidents in books as models, such as when the birds make a plan to save their tree in **LIZZIE AND THE BIRDS by Dawn Robertson**. In this example, the birds speak in bubbles but Lizzie's responses are in prose.

Linking to graphic novel formats and illustrated fiction

Share stories told in graphic novel formats where direct speech is sometimes written in ways other than bubbles, such as **NARWHAL UNICORN OF THE SEA by Ben Clanton**. If appropriate, compare and contrast to illustrated fiction books that tell a story through a combination of narration, cartoons and direct speech such as **ICED OUT by C. K. Smouha**. Point out other literary devices, such as thought bubbles and sound effects, using onomatopoeia e.g. *nom nom* for the sound of eating. Children often enjoy browsing graphic novels and illustrated fiction to search for and list common words used for sound effects.

KEY STAGE TWO EXAMPLE: A DREAM SEQUENCE

Key stage two children can work as a class and/or in groups to create an extra freeze-frame in a graphic novel in the form of a dream sequence. This context has the capacity to accommodate several speech or thought bubbles created by the children without changing the storyline. For example an extra dream frame for Monkey in **BUNNY VS MONKEY AND THE LEAGUE OF DOOM by Jamie Smart** might describe him having some new ideas to destroy the woodland creatures. Some graphic novels already have dream sequences that can be used as models e.g. Chapter 12 in **ROLLER GIRL by Victoria Jamieson**.

This work creates an opportunity for children to explore the features of graphic novels compared to other novels and experiment with some of the sequential art and literary devices used in the writing of graphic novels, such as the physical appearance of characters, mood colour, variations in size of print and frames, the use of sound effects and onomatopoeia, the impact of spacing and the use of narration boxes.

Links to reading

Graphic novels e.g.

BUNNY VS MONKEY AND THE LEAGUE OF DOOM by Jamie Smart
ROLLER GIRL by Victoria Jamieson
MR WOLF'S CLASS by Aron Nels Steinke (Yrs 3/4)

Illustrated novels using cartoon features e.g.

PIZAZZ by Sophy Henn
ICED OUT by C. K. Smouha (Yrs 3/4)

Texts for the Extension Activity e.g.

VARJAK PAW by S. F. Said
A SLEEPLESS NIGHT (Riding a Lion) by Coral Rumble

Planning and resources

- Select a page from a graphic novel that could potentially accommodate a dream as an extra frame without changing the storyline. This could be in the form of thought or speech bubbles where a character could reflect on recent events or on forthcoming events, such as the new pupils in Mr Wolf's class dreaming on the night before they meet their new teacher. Children will need sight of this page and the lead up to it during the lesson.
- Using other graphic novels and hybrids, select a few examples of literary devices like sound effects, onomatopoeia, zigzag frames and change of font size and capitalisation for emphasis. Children will need sight of these examples during the lesson.

You will need

- A space at the front of the class for one small group to perform;
- Space for small groups to plan and share freeze-frames;
- Individual whiteboards.

What to do

- If this is the first time children have attempted to write in graphic novel format, ask them to share their favourite comics with reasons why they like them. Then discuss any graphic novels they may have already read and the difference between a comic and a graphic novel. Talk about the use of sequential art in a graphic novel, where images tell most of the story, with dialogue and narration used to support the events.

- Introduce your chosen graphic novel and summarise the storyline up to the point where there could be an extra frame. Talk about the possibility of adding a dream sequence at this point in the narrative and what it might include. Encourage the children to consider how a character's dream might reflect recent events in the story. These can be ideas about what to do next, recollections of past events or fears about what others might say.
- Invite the children to talk about the features they would expect in a frame within a graphic novel. Use this as an opportunity to talk about the two forms of illustration in a graphic novel, namely foreground and background setting and discuss a possible setting for the dream that would fit in with this particular graphic novel.
- Invite a group of children to come to the front to make a freeze-frame representing the foreground image of the dream. This would be made up of the character and the 'voices' in the dream. Depending on the context, the voices may be real characters or disembodied voices. Each child representing a 'voice' should have a whiteboard with a speech bubble or thought bubble outline drawn on it.
- Decide whether the character in the frame would be lying down as if asleep or form part of the dream. Then ask the children to make suggestions on where the character and the speech or thought bubbles are positioned to create the best effect. If appropriate, look back at other frames to see if there is a pattern.
- Ask the class to suggest what could be written inside the bubbles and ask the 'voices' to write these inside their bubbles on the whiteboards. Add a sound effect as an extra bubble if appropriate to the context.
- Now make the freeze-frame, asking the voices to hold up their bubbles as if in a graphic novel frame. Children in the frame should hold the freeze as you read out the voice bubbles one at a time from left to right.
- Talk about how some words in graphic novels are enlarged or made bold for emphasis and ask the children if that might apply to any of the words in the bubbles in this freeze-frame.
- Ask the children how they read bubbles in graphic novels e.g. do they read from left to right as in a story or in a random order? Then repeat the freeze-frame and read the voices in a different order to assess the effect.
- Organise the children into small groups. Ask each group to create a freeze-frame of a dream portraying the foreground of an extra frame in a graphic/comic version of a well-known story such as a traditional fairy tale, a moment from the class novel or a moment from one of their own recent creations.
- Invite groups to share their completed freeze-frames with each other.
- Ask children to recreate one of their dream sequence freeze-frames on paper, as if they were writing a frame in a graphic novel. Ask them to create a suitable background as a setting for the foreground image. Use this as an opportunity to introduce and explore a range of other literary devices used in graphic novels e.g. the impact of the size and positioning of the frame in relation to the others and the use of colour to indicate mood and atmosphere. They can also consider using one or two of the onomatopoeia words used in graphic novels e.g. zoom, crash, thud, wack, etc.

Writers' reflections

- Ask the children if they find writing stories in a graphic novel format easier or more challenging to write than other stories and why they think this is.
- Talk about the skills needed by authors of graphic novels compared to other authors – what is the same and what is different?
- Use an illustrated novel to ask the children to pick out the similarities and differences between that novel and a graphic novel format.

Extension activities

- Compare the way dreams are communicated in graphic novels to the way dreams are handled in novels such as **VARJAK PAW by S. F. Said** and how poems about dreams are illustrated in poetry books such as **A SLEEPLESS NIGHT by Coral Rumble in *Riding a Lion*.**
- Using some of the literary devices from the lesson, children create a storyboard to plot the sequential art and write a page for a graphic novel incorporating a dream for a character in a well-known story or their own dream.
- Talk about the different types of graphic novels such as superheroes, realistic stories, autobiographies and historical events.
- Ask children to devise questions for an author of a graphic novel the children have read and contact the author to ask if the children can write to them or arrange a visit. Also, look for relevant resources on the author's website.

The one-minute playscript (key stage two)

Children learn how a playscript works by watching performances and by reading and performing plays, but learning how to write a good playscript is more challenging. Younger children often struggle to comprehend the difference between writing dialogue for a story and writing dialogue for a playscript and older children can become overwhelmed with the task of writing a full play. This can lead to poor-quality writing with insufficient time to address the features of a playscript and edit the work.

Writing a very short scripted scene lasting roughly one to two minutes when performed, however, means that both teacher and children have more time to concentrate on the features of a playscript and the quality of the writing. In addition, if children are given an opportunity to explore ideas for a scripted scene beforehand via improvisation, they are better able to visualise what the scripted version might look like when they come to write it. Composing and improvising a scene for a playscript, along with the promise of some kind of publication or performance, also creates a sense of ownership, along with a greater willingness to draft and edit the work.

54 *Drama as a Helping Hand*

KEY STAGE TWO EXAMPLE: WAITING, WAITING, WAITING

This example takes place over two or more lessons, but the Introductory lesson can be omitted or adapted if children already have an understanding of the features of a playscript compared to a narrative.

Links to reading

Text extracts that can be converted into playscripts e.g.

HORRID HENRY EATS A VEGETABLE, pp 1-5 (from *Horrid Henry's Underpants*) by Francesca Simon
GOODNIGHT MISTER TOM by Michelle Magorian, pp 9-10

Playscript versions of novels and traditional tales e.g.

- *THE BFG*: a play by David Wood
- *FANTASTIC MR FOX*: a play by Sally Reid
- *CHARLIE AND THE CHOCOLATE FACTORY*: a play by Richard George
- *DANNY CHAMPION OF THE WORLD*: a play by David Wood
- *JAMES AND THE GIANT PEACH*: a play by Richard George
- *THE TWITS*: a play by David Wood
- *THE WITCHES*: a play by David Wood
- *12 FABULOUSLY FUNNY FAIRY TALE PLAYS* by Justin Martin

Playscripts on different themes e.g.

- *PLAYTIME* by Julia Donaldson

Planning and resources

- Prepare a list of suggested contexts for the improvisations, based on the title *Waiting, Waiting, Waiting* e.g.
    - People at an event waiting for it to start, such as a sporting fixture, firework display, school play or music event.
    - People in a queue waiting for a fairground ride, a boat trip, entry to pets corner, a taxi, bus, train, ship or plane or maybe even a ride in a spaceship.
    - People in a waiting room at the vets, doctors, dentists or hairdressers.

You will need

For the optional introductory lesson:

- (Optional) A short clip of a film version of a familiar novel along with the parallel text e.g. the opening scene of **GOODNIGHT MISTER TOM by Michelle Magorian.**

Bubbles, comics and playscripts 55

- A short extract from a playscript version of a familiar story or novel that demonstrates the basic features of how a play is set out. Include the cast list and part of a scene with a few short speaking parts, a setting and some stage directions e.g. the start of Scene 4 in **Richard George's** adaptation of **CHARLIE AND THE CHOCOLATE FACTORY**. Some plays may also demonstrate how a narrator is used to replace or supplement any stage directions.
- A short extract from a text with a simple plot and dialogue that could easily be converted into a playscript format, such as the start of **HORRID HENRY EATS A VEGETABLE** from **HORRID HENRY'S UNDERPANTS by Francesca Simon** or the first two pages of **GOODNIGHT MISTER TOM by Michelle Magorian**.

For the drama:

- Enough space for groups of 3-4 children to create and perform their improvisations;
- A timer for yourself plus ideally one timer for each group;
- A screen for shared writing;
- Resources to make a class book of the children's completed scripts which can be either hand-written or typed.

What to do

(Optional) Introduction

- Ask children if they have seen film versions of novels or traditional stories and invite them to make comparisons. Talk about how a film version can be very different from the original story and how authors vary in how much they contribute to deciding what happens in the film. Then ask if any children have seen any theatrical play versions of stories and how pantomimes often have only a passing similarity to the story.
- Use the extract from the playscript version of a familiar novel or story to point out the differences between writing a story and writing a playscript. Use this extract as a model for the language as well as the features of a playscript e.g. the use of powerful adjectives and short sharp descriptions for the characters.
- Working as a whole class or with the children working in pairs, share the story extract and ask the children to convert it into a playscript version. Talk about the need for stage directions and other information that cannot be communicated via the dialogue.
- Make a copy of one playscript for one group to perform for the class. Then ask the class to compare it to the narrative version.

The drama

- Talk about how plays can be based on original ideas and improvisations, as well as versions of existing stories.
- Ask the children to work in groups, with each group creating a short, improvised scene to share with the class, before writing it as a playscript. Make it clear that whilst a play

is made up of several scenes organised into Acts, groups will be writing one short scene. Tell the children that their final scripts will be 'published' as a class book of short scenes.
- Organise children into groups of 3-5.
- Reveal the title of the improvisation as *Waiting, Waiting, Waiting* and share your list of suggestions. Invite the class to add suggestions to the list before asking each group to select one as a context for their improvisation.

Share the following guidance with the children, as appropriate

- The improvisation should be based on a conversation/dialogue rather than actions.
- Whilst children enjoy using props, they can prove to be a distraction, so apart from chairs and maybe a table, a *no props unless essential* rule is often the best option.
- All children should take part at whatever level they feel able and should be encouraged to take part. However, a child who finds it extremely stressful to speak in front of an audience can be offered a non-speaking part or help to direct the proceedings.
- The conversations between the actors in the improvisations should link to the subject of the play and fit in with school values. Some classes may need reminding of what would be considered inappropriate, such as bad language and comments that others may find upsetting or offensive.
- For safety reasons, actors should not make physical contact with each other or take part in dangerous actions. You may want to explain that professional actors take a long time to rehearse physical scenes and stunts so that no one gets hurt, but in school, there is no time to do this.
- Every improvisation must start and end with a freeze-frame and last between one and two minutes.

Rehearsals

- Move around the groups as they create and rehearse their improvisations. Support those who need help and encourage more confident groups to craft their work such as adding contrast and tension or humour. If groups have their own timers, encourage them to time their improvisations occasionally to check they are achieving but not exceeding the one- to two-minute duration.
- When most groups have finished, suggest a timed rehearsal for everyone. Those who have not finished can rehearse what they have done so far. Explain that you will time the rehearsals to allow a minimum of one minute and maximum of two minutes. Any performance over two minutes will need to stop.
- Ask all groups to start rehearsing their scenes simultaneously on the word *Action* from yourself. Groups who finish before the others should fold their arms and sit in silence until the two-minute deadline is up.
- Allow some time for groups whose improvisations are over or under the time limit to adapt their improvisations, whilst others improve theirs, ready for a script.
- Allow groups to share their completed improvisations with the rest of the class, but stress these may need to be adapted when converted into final scripts.

- Ask the audience to share one positive comment about each improvisation and one area that could be improved for the scripted version, adding your own suggestions if appropriate.

Writing the scripts

- Explain or remind the children how to set out a playscript, with information about the setting and the cast list, etc. Use this as an opportunity to explain how authors create, draft and then present their plays to an editor, who then suggests changes to ensure the play is good enough to be published. Explain that you will play the role of the editor for the forthcoming book of class plays to ensure a quality product that will appeal to a wide range of readers and performers. Using terminology from the real world of publishing in this way helps to engage the children by adding status to their forthcoming work.
  - **Option 1:** Children produce one script per group based on their improvisations. Each group should write a draft version for you to edit, before being allowed to write the final version for the book. Writing a script as a group, however short, requires a high level of co-operation, so if possible the task of scribe should be shared out amongst members of the group.
  - **Option 2:** Children write their own individual versions of their group improvisation, with help from others in their group if necessary. All the playscripts are then edited before being put together in the book. This means there will be a few versions of each play, but this provides an opportunity to comment on the similarities and differences in the various interpretations.

'Publishing/performing' the writing

- Ask children to suggest a cover design before making the completed scripts into a book for the class book corner.
- Add status to the work by placing the book alongside commercially produced plays in a section marked **PLAYS.**
- Make copies of at least one playscript from the class book for a group to perform. This can be achieved by reading lines from the copies or learning the lines by heart.

Writers' reflections

Explore some or all the following questions:

- Do you find it easier to write a play about a story you have made up and improvised or one based on an existing story?
- What is your view on playscript versions of novels? If you were an author of a novel, how would you feel about another author writing a playscript version?
- How does writing direct speech as a playscript compare to writing it as prose? Do you find one easier or more challenging than the other and if so, in what ways?

58   *Drama as a Helping Hand*

- How does writing direct speech as a playscript compare to writing it in a comic or graphic novel format? Which do you prefer to write and why? What are the main differences?

Extension activities

- Pairs first improvise and then script a short conversation between two characters from an existing story. This can be based on what happens in the story or what could potentially happen. Children write suitable short descriptions of the characters to add to their playscript.
- One or more scripts in the class book are adapted and recorded as an audio version, with added sound effects as an option. These can be placed in the book corner alongside the class book.
- The class selects one of their scripts for a group to perform in an assembly.
- Children convert part of their improvised storyline into a page for a graphic novel or illustrated fiction book and compare the two versions.
- Contact a playwright via their website to access information, background and any resources on writing plays.
- Take the children to see a live theatrical performance or an online version and ask them to write a short review of the plot, acting and stagecraft.

Silent movie scripts

Planning and resources

You will need

- (Optional) A short clip and information about silent movies;
- An acting area and a copy of the following summaries of scenes of the story of Cinderella as a model or another alternative:

  SCENE 1. In Cinderella's house
  Cinderella has to do all the work in the house. Her sisters are unkind to her. Her father ignores her. She is so tired that she often falls asleep in the kitchen.

  SCENE 2. One morning in the kitchen
  Cinderella receives an invitation to the ball at the palace. She is upset because she cannot go. Her fairy godmother appears and gives her a coach, a dress and glass slippers to go to the ball but she must be home by midnight.

  SCENE 3. At the ball
  Cinderella dances with the prince. Her sisters do not recognise her. They are jealous. At midnight Cinderella runs home but she drops her slipper. The prince picks it up.

  SCENE 4. A room in Cinderella's house the next day
  The prince and his servant arrive looking for the owner of the glass slipper. Every lady is asked to try it on. The sisters try it on but it doesn't fit. Cinderella tries it on and it fits. The prince asks her to marry him and she agrees. The end.

What to do

- Talk about silent movies and how they were often narrated in words but other versions include acting to a voiced narration. Show a clip if possible.
- Tell the children that you will narrate a silent movie version of Cinderella for some of the class to act. Invite children to play the characters. Ask them to wear name tags to identify themselves and/or use a simple item of clothing or a prop.
- Using the model of the story of Cinderella, narrate each scene and ask the children playing the characters to walk through the actions like a silent movie. This is meant to be fun and light-hearted but the actions must reflect the narrative as it is spoken fairly slowly. Run this twice so children gain a sense of what comes next and it flows.
- Ask children to write a modern version of Cinderella as a silent movie script.
- Then if appropriate, ask the children to work in groups to write part or all of another story in a silent movie script. This could be another fairy tale or an amusing, modern or alternative version of another traditional tale. Invite them to narrate their scripts as other children act them out as a silent movie. Alternatively, read out the scripts yourself to allow the groups to act in the scenes. Talk about cutting the story down to the bare essentials and provide some more examples if needed. Some groups may need to work on this as a class first before attempting one of their own.

Extension activity

- Children produce a booklet of silent movie scripts for the book corner and perform one in an assembly.

6 Write back

Opportunities for writing

Writing a reply to a letter and addressing a letter.

Contents

Write back key stage one examples	61
Goldilocks and the Three Bears	62
The Three Little Pigs	64
Further suggestions	66
The Three Billy Goats Gruff	66
The Owl Who Was Afraid of the Dark by Jill Tomlinson	66
Write back key stage two examples	66
Dog in the Playground by Allan Ahlberg	67
Matilda by Hilaire Belloc	70
Further suggestions	73
Beowulf by Charles Keeping	73
Lightning Falls by Amy Wilson	73
Mr Wolf's Class by Aron Nels Steinke	73

Drama strategies

Mantle-of-the-expert
Meet and Greet
Puppet-in-role
Role-on-the-wall
Teacher-in-role
Whole group drama

Overview

This chapter involves the teacher writing letters from characters linked to events in stories and narrative poems, in order to elicit a written response from the children in the form of a letter. They can be used as a stand-alone resource for children to write back either as themselves or in role as the recipients. However, the most effective way to use such letters is to incorporate some drama work, where children engage with the story or take on the roles of the recipients in a more active way. This encourages more imaginative written work with potential to motivate further reading and support recall.

The key stage one examples and further suggestions focus on simple stories or extracts to enable the children to concentrate on the writing rather than having to recall complicated events.

Write back key stage one examples

Example 1: GOLDILOCKS AND THE THREE BEARS
Example 2: THE THREE LITTLE PIGS

Further suggestions

THE THREE BILLY GOATS GRUFF
THE OWL WHO WAS AFRAID OF THE DARK by Jill Tomlinson

Links to reading

Texts

GOLDILOCKS AND THE THREE BEARS by Susanna Davidson (or any other traditional version)
THE THREE LITTLE PIGS by Nicola Baxter (or any other traditional version)
THE THREE LITTLE PIGS: AN ARCHITECTURAL TALE by Steve Guarnaccia
THE THREE BILLY GOATS GRUFF by Vera Southgate (or any other traditional version)
THE OWL WHO WAS AFRAID OF THE DARK by Jill Tomlinson

Stories with examples of written letters e.g.

BEANFEAST by Emma Yarlett
DEAR DINOSAUR by Chae Strathie
DEAR FAIRY GODMOTHER by Michael Rosen and Nick Sharratt
DEAR GREENPEACE by Simon Jam
DRAGON POST by Emma Yarlett
LETTERS FROM MAISIE by Lucy Cousins
THE DAY THE CRAYONS QUIT by Drew Daywalt and Oliver Jeffers
THE JOLLY POSTMAN by Janet and Allan Ahlberg
YOURS TRULY, GOLDILOCKS by Alma Flor Ada

Stories with postcards e.g.

MEERKAT MAIL by Emily Gravett
WISH YOU WERE HERE by Martina Selway

62   *Drama as a Helping Hand*

KEY STAGE ONE EXAMPLE 1: GOLDILOCKS AND THE THREE BEARS

Planning and resources

Children need to be familiar with the main events in the story of Goldilocks and the Three Bears and have access to a written version e.g. **GOLDILOCKS AND THE THREE BEARS by Susanna Davidson.**

You will need

- Space at the front of the class for four children to stand in a freeze-frame;
- A large unused envelope and a few used envelopes with the addresses clearly written on the fronts;
- A hand-written copy of the following letter:

3 Forest Lane
Storytown
ST1 3GB

Dear children

> *I hear you are very kind and I wonder if you could help me. My little girl is called Goldilocks and last week she did a very silly thing. She went into the forest on her own without telling me. She hadn't even had her breakfast. I was very worried and went to look for her, but I couldn't find her. When I came home Goldilocks was waiting for me outside our door. Her dress was covered in something that looked like porridge and she was looking very scared. When I asked her where she had been, she wouldn't tell me. I think she may have done something naughty, but I'm not sure.*
> *My neighbour says they saw Goldilocks walking towards the Three Bears' house, but Goldilocks doesn't know the bears, so I don't think she went to their house.*
> *If you know anything about what happened please would you write and let me know.*
> *I look forward to hearing from you.*

> *Best wishes*
> *From Goldilocks' Mummy*

NB: Substitute the name of another carer for *Goldilocks' Mummy* if more appropriate.

What to do

- Read and/or remind children about the end of the story of Goldilocks and the Three Bears, when Goldilocks runs out of their house back into the forest.
- Ask four children to represent the bears and Goldilocks in a freeze-frame of the moment the bears watch Goldilocks run away. Involve the class in the decisions about where the characters would be positioned and how they would be feeling. Then make the freeze-frame using a narrative introduction e.g.

    This is what it might have looked like when Goldilocks ran out of the bears' house ... Freeze... 1,2,3... relax.

- Invite children to speculate about where Goldilocks would be going as she ran away and if she would tell anyone about what she did when she got home. Talk about how her parents or carers might feel if they found out how naughty she had been and what they might say to her.
- Ask them to pretend that Goldilocks' Mummy (or whoever is named on the letter) has written them a letter, asking them about what happened. Bring out the letter and read it to the children.
- Check they understand the letter by reading it again after feigning confusion and then ask them to clarify what they need to do.
- Work with the children to draft a reply to the letter, covering the main points. If appropriate, use this as an opportunity to talk about the features of a letter and the text structures of sequencing and describing in order to offer an explanation.
- When the letter is complete, read it back to the children and invite them to comment. Make any necessary adaptations to the letter and then show the children the envelope you will put it in. If you have made a large or digital copy of the letter, offer to write it on paper so it can fit inside the envelope. After checking the letter for the correct address, refer to the used envelopes to demonstrate how an address should be organised on an envelope. After writing the address on the envelope with the help of the children, offer to buy a stamp and post it later.
- After a few days, write a reply from Goldilocks' Mummy thanking the children for their letter.
- Praise the children for their letter-writing skills as well as their kindness and ideas.

Writers' reflections

- Share other real-life experiences of writing and receiving letters.
- Link to stories involving the writing of letters.
- Talk about the difference between writing a letter and writing a postcard and link to books with models of postcards.

Extension activity

Suggest that Goldilocks could make up for her behaviour by writing a letter of apology to the bears and maybe offering to do jobs in the house or play with Baby Bear. Then let the children write individual letters to Goldilocks with their suggestions on what she could do or write a composite letter, summarising their ideas. Place the reply or replies in another envelope and ask the children to check the address and how it is written.

After a few days, tell the children that you have had a phone call from Goldilocks' Mummy thanking the children for their ideas. Explain that Goldilocks took their advice and the bears are now her friends.

KEY STAGE ONE EXAMPLE 2: THE THREE LITTLE PIGS

Planning and resources

- Children need to be familiar with the main events in the story of The Three Little Pigs and have access to a written version e.g. **THE THREE LITTLE PIGS by Nicola Baxter.**
- Make a copy of the following letter:

Jones the Builders
3 The Builders Yard
Storytown
ST1 PW5

Dear Children

I wonder if you can help me find out what has happened to the 3 pigs, who asked me for building materials a while ago. I have heard people around here saying that the pigs have been in some kind of trouble with a wolf. I am very worried about them and I am keen to help them if I can.

I met the first little pig a few weeks ago. He asked me for some straw to build his house. I warned him that straw was not going to be strong enough for a house, but he still wanted it, so I gave him some.

Did the first little pig ever build his house with my straw?

Do you know what happened to him?

If you do please write back and let me know.

I met the second little pig the next day. He asked me for some wood to build his house. I told him that, even though wood was stronger than straw, it was not the best thing to build a house with. Anyway, he said he still wanted the wood, so I gave him some.

Did the second little pig ever build his house with my wood?

Do you know what happened to him?

If you do please write back and let me know.

I met the third little pig later that same day and he asked for some bricks to build his house. I told him that bricks were the best materials for building houses and I told him he had made a good choice. I gave him some bricks and he thanked me and went away.

Did the third little pig ever build his house with my bricks?

Do you know what happened to him?

If you do please write back and let me know.

I hope the 3 pigs are alright. Please write back soon.

Best wishes from
Mr Jones the builder

NB: Replace the name *Jones* with a name the children would be more familiar with if appropriate.

You will need

- A blank envelope for the reply to the letter;
- A used envelope with an address and a stamp on it;
- A small glove puppet;
- A copy of the story of The Three Little Pigs e.g. **THE THREE LITTLE PIGS by Nicola Baxter**.

What to do

- Ask the children if they can pretend to be in a story with a puppet.
- Bring out the puppet and make it appear to be excited about something. The puppet communicates by whispering to you, so you can then tell the children what it says.
- The puppet is excited because it has just phoned Jones the Builders to talk about a new house it is having built. The puppet is not sure whether to have its house built of straw, wood or bricks and asks the children what they think. The puppet then asks the children if they know what happened to three pigs who built houses of straw, wood and bricks, and if so they can help the builder with some information.
- Let the puppet bring out the letter from Jones the Builders addressed to the children and then put the puppet away so it can think more about its house.
- Read the letter from Jones the Builders to the children and help them draft a reply covering all the questions. Refer to the story to check the details. If appropriate, use this as an opportunity to talk about the features of a letter and the text structures of sequencing and describing involved in writing explanations.
- Bring the puppet back to ask if the children have replied to the letter. Let the children help you read the letter to the puppet to check it makes sense. Let the puppet comment on the clarity of the letter and praise the children for their efforts.
- If you have used a large piece of paper, offer to rewrite the letter later so it's small enough to go in an envelope.
- Bring out the envelope and check the builder's address, before writing it. Show the children an addressed stamped envelope and talk about how to arrange the address on an envelope and where to put the stamp.
- Tell the children that you are now going to tell them what happened next: *when the builder got the letter, he was very pleased and phoned the children's teacher to thank them.* Announce that this is the end of the story of how some children from (name your class) helped a builder understand what happened to The Three Little Pigs.

Writers' reflections

- Ask the children if they think their letter was a good letter and if so why. Link and compare their letter to other letters in stories.
- Talk about the difference between a letter and a postcard and use examples in stories as models.

Extension activities

- The puppet asks the children for some ideas on what kind of house it should build. The puppet asks them to write down their ideas so it can think about them all. Children then write a plan or picture of a house for the puppet, with a written note about the best materials for the walls, doors and windows. After the activity, bring the puppet back to collect the ideas and thank the children.
- Read children an alternative version of the story with different building materials such as **THE THREE LITTLE PIGS: AN ARCHITECTURAL TALE by Steve Guarnaccia.**

Further suggestions

- **THE THREE BILLY GOATS GRUFF:** after reading a version of the story e.g. **LADYBIRD TALES: THE THREE BILLY GOATS GRUFF by Vera Southgate,** the children create a Role-on-the-wall for the Troll. They write what they know about the Troll from the story inside the outline and add what they imagine the Troll might be like around the outside. They then receive a letter from someone living near the bridge where the Troll used to live. This person has heard a rumour that the Troll is no longer there. They can't believe it and write to the children asking if they know whether the rumour is true or not and if so how it could have happened.
- **THE OWL WHO WAS AFRAID OF THE DARK by Jill Tomlinson:** after using a teacher-in-role or a puppet-in-role to hot-seat Plop about his meeting with the old lady who told Plop that dark was kind, the children receive a letter from the lady. She would like to know if Plop ever cured his fear of the dark and if so, how did he do it.

Write back key stage two examples

Example 1: DOG IN THE PLAYGROUND
Example 2: MATILDA

Further suggestions

- *BEOWULF*
- *LIGHTNING FALLS*
- *MR WOLF'S CLASS*

Links to reading

Texts

- *DOG IN THE PLAYGROUND* by Allan Ahlberg
    - (Extension Activity) *I COSMO* by Carlie Sorosiak
    - (Extension Activity) *DOG DIARIES* by Steven Butler

- *MATILDA* by Hilaire Belloc
- *BEOWULF* by Charles Keeping and Kevin Crossley-Holland
- *LIGHTNING FALLS* by Amy Wilson
- *MR WOLF'S CLASS* by Aron Nels Steinke

Books which include letters e.g.

- *DEAR TEACHER* by Amy Husband (Yrs 3/4)
- *THE DRAGON SITTER'S SURPRISE* by Josh Lacey (Yrs 3/4)
- *TO NIGHTOWL FROM DOGFISH* by Holly Goldberg-Sloan and Meg Wolitzer (Yrs 5/6)
- *THE LAST POST* by Keith Campion (Yrs 5/6)
- *A SONG FOR WILL* by Hilary Robinson (Yrs 5/6)

KEY STAGE TWO EXAMPLE 1: DOG IN THE PLAYGROUND

Planning and resources

All children need access to the poem **DOG IN THE PLAYGROUND by Allan Ahlberg.**

You will need

- Individual whiteboards;
- A scarf or tie to represent a teacher;
- Space for children to walk around in pairs and talk to each other;
- An official-looking copy of the following letter, with the name of your town added to the address:

R.S.P.C.D Royal Society for the Prevention of Cruelty to Dogs
Complaints Dept.
5 Long Road
Abbeytown
AB5 8YT

Re: Investigation of an alleged incident of cruelty to a stray dog
Dear Head Teacher

We are investigating an alleged incident of cruelty to a stray dog, in your school playground. We are not able to divulge the name of the person who made the complaint, but we can tell you that it came from someone outside your school, who witnessed the incident in the playground.

Under the law, we have the power to prosecute anyone who is cruel to defenceless animals. We understand from our witness, that a stray dog was taken into school by one of the pupils. The witness could not see what was happening inside the school building but heard children and staff screaming and shouting at the poor dog in the playground. It is alleged that a large group of children and several staff chased the poor frightened dog around the playground and pelted it with stones to make it go away. The injured dog was last seen running out of the playground gates in a very distressed condition.

We would like to give you the opportunity to respond to this allegation and provide us with your version of events. We need your accounts in writing at the earliest opportunity.

Please provide as much detail as possible, as you may need to defend yourself should we decide to prosecute.

Please send your detailed account(s) to the RSPCD office and mark it for the attention of The Complaints Department.

Yours sincerely
Zillah Harris
RSPCD Investigating Officer

What to do

- Read the poem to the children a couple of times to familiarise them with the sequence of events in the poem when a dog appeared in a school playground.
- Ask the children to imagine that the school in the poem was their school and that they were some of the children who witnessed the dog coming into their classroom. Mention that the poem doesn't give details of what happened in the classroom, but we know that the dog didn't harm anyone or cause any hygiene issues. Ask the children to suggest what they might have witnessed and add some ideas yourself if necessary e.g. the dog may have been in the art cupboard among the paints, in the book corner among the cushions or had its head in the waste paper basket, etc.
- Working in pairs or threes, ask the children to invent something they saw the dog doing that day and make a note of it on a whiteboard. Encourage them to think of an incident that would fit with the tone of the rest of the poem such as something funny, chaotic or surprising.

Meet and Greet

- Explain the following **Meet and Greet** activity: on the word *Action*, pairs will walk around the room meeting and greeting other pairs. Each pair should tell whomever they meet what they saw the dog doing in the classroom and listen to what the other pairs saw. They should talk in role as the children in the poem; starting with the words *we saw the dog...* The activity will stop on the word *Freeze*, when the children will be asked to sit down again. They will then be asked how many incidents they can remember about what the dog did in the classroom. This encourages them to listen to others as they move around.
- Before starting the activity, ask pairs to decide how they will tell their story i.e. either one of the pair will talk or they take turns. They can use the whiteboard as a prompt if they wish.
- Start the Meet and Greet activity and run it just long enough for each pair to explain their story two or three times. Keep the feedback short and praise those who demonstrate good listening skills.

Whole group drama

- Ask the children to take on the roles of the children in the poem for a drama activity. Set the scene in the classroom, a few days after the event with the dog. Explain that their class teacher was away on the day the dog came into school and the drama starts when the teacher asks them to explain what happened.
- Ask the children to accept you could be that teacher when you wear the scarf or tie. Give yourself a different name and write it on a board so they can remember it.
- Use the words *Action* and *Freeze* to start and stop the drama.
- Start the drama by taking on the role of the class teacher asking the children what happened when the dog came into the classroom. Listen to a few ideas then ask what happened in the playground and if the dog was OK.
- Then tell the children that the head teacher has had a very upsetting letter from the RSPCD and has asked you to read it to them.
- Read the letter to the children and then ask them if they have anything to say. Try to encourage the children to address the accusations and consider how they will refute them in their required witness statements.
- Suggest they work with you to write a formal letter of reply to explain what happened. Base the evidence on the events in the poem and the experiences the children created as eyewitnesses. Use this as an opportunity to focus on the features of a formal letter and the text structures of sequencing and describing used in written explanations.
- Stop the drama and take off the scarf or tie to come out of role as the teacher.
- Invite the children to conclude the story of the drama by writing the reply to the letter from the RSPCD. The general letter can be composed as a whole class, with pairs or individuals writing their own accounts of what happened. Use this as an opportunity for children to reply to a formal letter requesting information. Encourage them to deal with each point politely but clearly and concisely.
- Tell the children that you are going to tell them what happened next in the story of the drama.

    Narrate the following: *the head teacher was pleased with the reply composed by the children and sent it off to the RSPCD the next day. After a week, the head teacher received a phone call to say that the accusation of cruelty to a dog at the school had been dropped, due to the overwhelming evidence provided by the children. The head teacher thanked the children in assembly and gave the children the news that the dog who caused so much trouble was safe and well and had now been returned to its owner.*

Writers' reflections

- Ask the children how they felt in the drama when they were wrongly accused and if their feelings made the reply more difficult or easier to write. Talk about whether feeling deeply about something makes you write differently.
- Talk about the difference between writing formal and informal letters and link to books with letters on serious topics e.g. **THE LAST POST by Keith Camion** and ***A SONG FOR WILL* by Hilary Robinson**.

- Talk about how letters can reveal an unfolding story and refer to specific texts as examples if appropriate.
- Talk about when people might need to write and/or reply to formal letters in real life.

Extension activities

- Using Allan Ahlberg's poem as a model, children write their own poems or stories about a different animal in the playground.
- Children write a letter to the RSPCA and/or a local dog's home asking for information about their work.
- Children write a version of the events in Allan Ahlberg's poem from the dog's perspective. Link to texts where dogs are narrators such as *I COSMO* by **Carlie Sorosiak** and *DOG DIARIES* by **Steven Butler.**

KEY STAGE TWO EXAMPLE 2: MATILDA

Planning and resources

- Children will need access to the text of the poem **MATILDA by Hilaire Belloc** at the beginning of the lesson and another version with illustrations at the end.
- Make an official-looking copy of the following letter:

From The Daily Herald Newspaper
To the people living in Matilda's street

Dear residents

Please give this letter your urgent attention.

Our newspaper, the Daily Herald, will soon be writing an article about what happened to the young girl called Matilda, whose house was burned down in your street recently. But before we write the article, we feel it is only fair to ask you for your side of the story.

We can't understand why neighbours such as yourselves, would ignore the cries of a young girl as she screamed for help from an open window. The fire started in the early evening, so it's likely most of you were at home and some of you would be passing her house on your way home from work. If you were passing by at that time, you certainly would have seen her hanging out of her window, calling for help. Even if you were at home, you would have heard her shouting 'Fire' at the top of her voice.

Why no one called the fire brigade is a complete mystery to us all here at the newspaper office.

*It seems that, by the time Matilda's aunt returned from her visit to the theatre, the house was already burnt, so **she** cannot be blamed for not calling the fire brigade.*

By the way, when we interviewed members of the fire brigade about this case, one of them thought they had been to Matilda's house before, but on that occasion, it turned out to be a hoax call. Do you know if this was true? Do any of you remember seeing a fire engine at Matilda's house when there was no fire?

We have to warn you that the people of the town are saying that you are heartless neighbours, who did nothing to save a young girl trapped by fire. We intend to publish our article on the Matilda case within the next 2 weeks, so if you want us to put your side of the story, we advise you to write back as soon as possible.

Yours sincerely
M. Shaw
Editor of the Daily Herald

You will need

- Space at the front of the class for a small group to make a freeze-frame.

What to do

- Read the text of the poem to the children, without showing them any illustrations and ask them to follow it as you read.
- Then ask the children to imagine they were Matilda's neighbours. Explain that this role-play work will help them study the poem in greater detail.
- Explain that you would like the children to illustrate what the neighbours saw, using a freeze-frame instead of a drawing.
- Set the freeze-frame to represent the moment when the crowd was cheering the fire brigade, after Matilda's hoax call. Explain that the freeze-frame must illustrate what the neighbours were doing and saw at that time and reflect the relevant lines in the poem.
- Clear a small space for a performance area. Make sure that all children can see into the space from where they are sitting.
- Designate an area at the side or back of the space to represent the front of Matilda's house and the windows. Make it clear that the freeze-frame represents the view the neighbours had from their houses across the street or from where they were standing as part of the crowd looking up at the windows. Ask them to imagine that the ladders were placed up at the windows with firemen starting to climb them.
- Choose two children to represent those neighbours looking at Matilda's windows from their houses across the street and place them across from Matilda's windows. Then ask the class to decide how these neighbours might be positioned. Ask some questions for them to consider such as: Were they standing or sitting? Were they looking with hands to their faces, shielding their eyes for a better view, using binoculars or waving?
- Now ask the rest of the children in the class to represent the neighbours standing in the crowd. Ask the class to decide how the crowd might be positioned if they were cheering and frenzied, as it says in the poem.
- On the count of *1,2,3 Freeze*, ask everyone to make the freeze-frame. They should hold the freeze whilst you read the corresponding lines and then say *relax*.
- Explain that when they make the freeze-frame again, some of the neighbours will be invited to speak out about what they might be thinking. Ask the class to provide some

suggestions. Encourage children to think about the neighbours' perspective and the risk to their own houses. Suggest that some may have heard about Matilda telling lies and may be suspicious and some may also have seen her aunt going out, leaving Matilda alone and bored and they may have thoughts about this.
- Make it clear that they can either use these suggestions or make up their own thoughts. Give children a few minutes to talk in pairs to decide what they might be thinking as a neighbour.
- After the count of three as before, ask the children to make the freeze-frame again but explain that when you point to them they should articulate their thoughts. Either point to all the neighbours in turn or select a few, depending on the size of the class. They should not break the freeze until you say *relax*.
- (Optional) Ask the children to draw/sketch an illustration of the neighbours listening to Matilda shouting *Fire* on the night of the real fire. They should include a thought bubble. Make it clear that their illustration should illustrate the following lines from the poem:

For every time she shouted 'Fire'
They only answered 'Little Liar!'

Using the letter from The Daily Herald

- Ask the children to continue to take on the role of Matilda's neighbours. Ask them to imagine that they all received a copy of a letter from *The Daily Herald*. Read and/or show them a copy of the letter and then help them to devise a written response as neighbours. This could be in the form of one letter from the class as if from a residents' group, a few letters from groups as if from families, or letters from individual neighbours.
- Then working individually or in pairs, ask children to write the article they would want to see in *The Daily Herald* about Matilda and the fire. They could make up a suitable headline or use **Matilda: The whole truth**. Children then sketch an accompanying newspaper photograph.

Writers' reflections

Invite the children to consider the difference; if the neighbours had been asked to defend themselves via an interview with a journalist instead of having time to write a letter. Invite them to compare the immediacy of the spoken word to the considered process of writing a letter.

Extension activity

- Children write two short diary entries in role as one of the neighbours. The first entry was made on the night of the hoax call, and the second entry was made on the night of the real fire.

Further suggestions

- **BEOWULF by Charles Keeping and Kevin Crossley Holland:** Beowulf is about to select a group of the best warriors to accompany him on his voyage to slay Grendel, but before he does, he needs evidence of their bravery. A written message arrives from Beowulf, asking prospective warriors for their stories of bravery. Groups of children in role as warriors produce freeze-frames of their bravest deeds before each warrior writes back to Beowulf describing their part in the event.
- **LIGHTNING FALLS by Amy Wilson:** Children in role as past visitors to the Lightening Falls Hotel, receive a letter from the online company Hotel Adviser asking if they can recommend it. Children work in pairs to create memories of their visit. They then share them with other pairs in a Meet and Greet activity, before replying in writing to Hotel Adviser along with a star rating.
- **MR WOLF'S CLASS by Aron Nels Steinke:** Principal Wilox, the Head teacher of Hazelwood School receives a letter from the parent of a new child who is worried about the prospect of joining a class with a wolf as the teacher. The head asks the pupils in Mr Wolf's class to share their experiences, so a reply can be sent. After composing a Role-on-the-wall for Mr Wolf as a whole class, individuals or pairs write back in role as one of the pupils.

PART II
Drama as a Compelling Context

Part II

Drama and Communities

7 An imaginary community
Key stage one and lower key stage two

Contents	
Key stage one example: Pets corner	78
Key stage one/lower key stage two example: A beautiful place	80

Drama strategies

Freeze-frames
Performing actions to an audience
Role-play area
Teacher as narrator
Teacher-in-role
Whole group drama

Overview

Creating an imaginary community at key stage one and lower key stage two can accommodate a wide range of contexts for learning, including writing. The term community encompasses a wide range of contexts, including people living in a street, a block of flats, a village, a town, an island, a castle, an undiscovered planet or a magic city. It can also include people working in a park, fairground or other public space.

The drama can be based on a community in a story, such as imaginary inhabitants on the Isle of Struay in **KATY MORAG'S ISLAND STORIES by Mairi Hedderwick,** or based on inhabitants involved in a real-life event such as The Great Fire of London.

The community itself can be developed from a basic given outline or created entirely by the children. Most contexts have the potential to provide a range of opportunities for writing but what tends to motivate the writing is not so much the context, as the sense of ownership and belonging created by the drama. A strong sense of ownership will help motivate children to complete related writing tasks.

KEY STAGE ONE EXAMPLE: PETS CORNER

Opportunities for writing

Descriptive writing for information, instructions, lists and recount/narrative.

Planning and resources

You will need

- A hall or cleared space for the drama activities;
- Small whiteboards for the drama;
- Information about different pets and how to look after them;
- (Optional) Photos of a Pets Corner;
- An area in the classroom to represent the Pets Corner shop and information centre.

What to do

PART A: BUILDING BELIEF

In the hall or cleared space

NB: This example is based on a Pets Corner, but it could easily be adapted for an animal or bird sanctuary or a farm area.

Making the contract and defining the space

- Ask the children if they can join you in a drama by pretending to be the people who work in a Pets Corner in a park. Talk about and share resources about Pets Corners and what kinds of pets they might have to look after.
- Working in pairs or small groups, ask children to decide what pet they will look after in the drama about Pets Corner. Ask groups to tell everyone what pet they have chosen and make a list. If more than a couple of groups choose similar pets, suggest some groups look after an extra, different kind of pet to make Pets Corner more interesting.
- Talk about what kind of environment each pet needs and why some pets need to be kept away from others for their own safety.
- Ask each group to write the name of their pet on a whiteboard so visitors will know what they are.
- Talk about the jobs the workers will need to do to look after each pet before asking groups to decide what jobs they will do when the drama begins. Make sure everyone is responsible for at least one pet and at least one job.
- Ask the children to imagine that the hall is the Pets Corner. Define exactly what part of the hall is to be used and specify any items or PE equipment not in the drama.
- Talk about the best place for each kind of pet to be located and then ask the groups to write the name of their pet on their whiteboard and sit in the appropriate area for their pet with the whiteboard on display or on a chair.

- Explain that the drama will start on an ordinary day before the visitors arrive when the workers arrive to look after their pets. Explain that all the jobs need to be mimed but they can talk as if they were really the workers. Demonstrate how a few jobs might be mimed and ask children to suggest other mimes.
- Allow groups time to think about what jobs they will do when the drama starts and how they might mime them.
- Explain that the drama will start on the word *Action* and stop on the word *Freeze*. Tell the children that when you say the word *Action* each group should pretend to arrive at work in Pets Corner and carry out their jobs.

Dramatic play

- Let this run for as long as most children are engaged. Move around the groups in role as one of the workers, asking if anyone needs any help or if there are any problems.
- Stop the drama with the word *Freeze* and then ask half of the class to show the others the jobs they were doing by performing some of their actions again. This performance should last only a few minutes before the audience is asked to guess the kind of jobs they see. Then swap over so the other half of the class can perform their jobs in the same way.
- Tell the children that this is the end of this first part of the drama and ask them to bring their whiteboards to the side of the room so you can all sit and talk.

Reflection

- Ask the children if they enjoyed looking after their pets in the drama. Ask them if there were any problems and how their pets behaved. Explain that visitors might need more information and safety instructions about feeding pets than just the names of the pets. They will need to write these before the next drama.

Writing in the classroom

'Publishing' the writing

- Ask the children to pretend that a corner of the classroom is an information centre for Pets Corner where visitors can go to find out about the pets.
- Ask individuals or groups to write information about their pets for the centre. This can be a simple poster made up of a few sentences or a leaflet with illustrations. Talk about what information needs to be included e.g. what the pet looks like, what it eats, how to look after it, etc. Provide access to appropriate resources to enable this as necessary.
- Bring the class together and talk about any safety rules that need to be written for the visitors. These can be made by groups or composed by the class.
- Talk about how to keep the pets safe and what they would need to do if one of the pet houses was damaged and a pet escaped or there was a flood. Make a plan of what to do in an emergency such as closing off any escape routes, taking pets to another area for safety or sending search parties out. Make a list for the workers entitled 'What To Do In An Emergency.'
- Ask children to write a few sentences describing what jobs they do to look after the pets. This can be in the form of a booklet or poster for the information centre entitled 'How We Look After Pets Corner' or 'Meet The People Who Look After Pets Corner.'

PART B: THE PROBLEM
The problem can be anything that could happen in a Pets Corner e.g. a visitor could claim that one of the pets scared them causing the workers to review their safety procedures or someone might complain that there are not enough pets for young children to stroke, causing the workers to consider buying more and deciding on which pets are best. The following example refers to problems caused by a storm:

- Restart the drama with a meeting of the workers to inform them that a storm has blown down some barriers between pet areas, and some of the pets have escaped. Rain has also been leaking into some pet houses so the pets need to be moved. Talk about where they could rehouse the pets if necessary and refer to their list of 'What To Do In An Emergency.' Check that everyone knows what to do and send them off to rescue the pets and rehouse them.
- Let this run for as long as children are engaged and join in with the rescue as one of the workers. Then call everyone back for another meeting, asking workers to report back on what happened.
- Praise the workers for all their work and tell them that the pets are all now safe.
- Tell them that Pets Corner can soon open again but damage from the storm needs repairing first. Talk about what kind of damage they might find.
- Ask the workers to get tools from the sheds around the park and look for anything that needs repairing.
- Let this run for a while before calling a meeting so everyone can report back on what they've repaired.
- Thank the workers for saving Pets Corner from the storm. Then stop the drama.

Writing in the classroom

- Ask children to write about their experiences in solving the problems caused by the storm. This can be made into a booklet for the class book corner entitled 'How We Saved Pets Corner.'

Extension activities

- Children make other small items for visitors to Pets Corner, such as bookmarks with a drawing of the pet and a sentence about it.
- Link to stories about pets and information books about how to look after them.

KEY STAGE ONE/LOWER KEY STAGE TWO EXAMPLE: A BEAUTIFUL PLACE

Opportunities for writing

Descriptive writing and explanations; writing letters and writing persuasive text.

An imaginary community: Key stage one and lower key stage two   81

Overview

This works best with children in Years 2-4 but can easily be simplified or made more complex for other age groups.

The drama is designed to be spread over more than one drama lesson with classroom time in between to complete the writing. A classroom display or small role-play area representing a Visitors Centre and/or a gift or book shop is advisable as a means of publishing the writing.

The name of the beautiful place is optional but needs to reflect the desirability for visitors. Either choose the name yourself or invite children to make suggestions and decide via a vote. The beautiful place in this example has been named as Sunny Park.

Planning and resources

You will need

- Resources to create a large portable sketch map with the children, based on a simple outline of a river across the centre of the map crossed at two points by bridges, a Visitors Centre at the bottom of the map and a small section of woodland on the opposite side to the Visitors Centre. You may want to use the correct geographical symbols for the bridges and woods. Write the name of the place above the map and name the Visitors Centre to give it status e.g. SUNNY PARK VISITORS CENTRE;
- A display area in the classroom to represent The Visitors Centre;
- A hall or cleared space with a place to display the map;
- Two or three large, preferably blue, PE mats to represent the river in the hall;
- A scarf or jacket as a sign of teacher-in-role.

What to do

There are two ways to create a map of a beautiful place. One is to create it with the children in the classroom before the drama and the other is to sketch it as the children create it during the drama. Either is feasible but in this particular example, the map is created in the classroom beforehand.

PART A: BUILDING BELIEF

Preparation in the classroom

- Show the children the outline map of Sunny Park and describe it as a beautiful place for families to visit. Mention the Visitors Centre where this map is displayed along with other information about Sunny Park.
- Mention the sparseness and invite the children to add more attractions and beautiful things to attract more visitors. Explain that they will be using this map in some drama work at a later time.
- Invite a few suggestions from the whole class before organising the children into groups of three to decide on two to four things they would like to add to the map. Explain that they need to have more than one idea in case another group chooses the same thing.

- Ask groups to prioritise their lists before making their suggestions. Consider each idea before asking each group where they would like their attraction to be sited and then record it onto the map using a symbol. Use this as an opportunity to illustrate why we need symbols rather than full pictures on a map. Try not to influence the children's suggestions if they are offered with integrity. A beautiful attractive place for children may not be the same as for an adult. However, any unrealistic attractions, such as a full-sized football ground, need to be challenged and a compromise suggested such as a small area for football training with a resident coach. Some groups will likely choose the same attraction, so if this is the case children should choose another from their list unless the class feels they need more than one. For example, a play park is a very common suggestion and the children may want more than one. If children suggest walks or trails, then identify the place to start and use broken lines to indicate the route.
- Ask the children what kind of boundary Sunny Park should have, trees, fence, walls, etc., and where the main entrance would be located. Mark these on the map as appropriate.
- When the map is completed ask the children to write a sentence or a short paragraph describing their group's chosen attraction for a booklet in the Visitors Centre book and gift shop. They can also provide a sketch if appropriate.
- Suggest they make a version of the Sunny Park book and gift shop in the classroom. Place the descriptions in a booklet and place it in the Sunny Park shop in the classroom. Talk about what else they might add to the shop in the future.

Drama in the hall

Making the contract and defining the space

- Sit the children together on the floor but in the same groups as in the classroom. Ask the children if they will play the parts of some visitors to Sunny Park to see what they think of the attractions. Their feedback will help to advertise the place.
- Allocate a side of the room to represent the Visitors Centre and ask the children to sit there as if they were inside the building looking out of a large window into Sunny Park towards the river with the woods beyond. Place the map somewhere in the Visitor's Centre so children can see it from where they are sitting.
- Place the PE mats in a line across the middle of the hall to represent the river. Leave gaps between them for the bridges. Explain this to the children and point out where the woods would be situated in relation to the river.
- Make it clear that whatever they decide to do in Sunny Park needs to be mimed. Choose a couple of attractions and suggest how they could be mimed such as stepping backwards and forwards to mime being on a swing. Ask the children for a couple more ideas for miming other attractions. Make it clear that whilst actions are mimed, the children should talk as if they were really the visitors. If any of the attractions involve the river such as boating or swimming, etc. then ask the children to use the floorspace alongside the mats rather than use the mats themselves which may slip. Look out for any other likely problems that may occur when miming and negotiate a solution e.g. miming playing ball games in a designated area so it's not dangerous for others and miming

An imaginary community: Key stage one and lower key stage two 83

swimming in the river alongside the mats rather than on them and perhaps involve walking whilst miming swimming strokes rather than lying on the floor.
- Point out any areas of the hall that will not be used in the drama such as wall bars, any PE equipment or chairs.

Dramatic play

- Go through the attractions in turn on the map and ask the children where each would be located in the hall in relation to the river, Visitors Centre and woods.
- Allow groups a few minutes to decide which two attractions they will visit during the drama and which they will visit first.
- Explain that the drama will start with a freeze-frame of the moment when everyone was just about to start their first activity. On the word *Action*, the freeze-frame will come to life as if on a video and continue until you say the word *Freeze*. In order to prepare for this, allow groups a few minutes to decide where they will be located for the freeze-frame and how their bodies will be positioned for the freeze. Encourage the children to choose positions they can hold for a short while. Offer a few suggestions beforehand if necessary e.g. *you might be walking towards something, have your hand in your pocket for money to buy ice cream at the café, or have your hand raised to stroke an animal in Pets Corner.*
- Reinforce the idea that they should talk to each other as if they were really there and move to another activity when they finish the first one. Remind them that the map is in the Visitors Centre if they wish to look at it to see where to go next.
- Ask groups to walk into their frozen positions a few at a time until everyone is frozen. Wait for everyone to be still and then say *Action* to start the dramatic play. Let this run for a few minutes or for as long as most children appear to be engaged.
- Stop the drama on the word *Freeze* and select groups to return to their original places in the Visitors Centre a few at a time until all groups are there.

Performing to consolidate and add status

- Select about half the groups to return to their frozen starting positions in Sunny Park and ask them to show the rest of the class some of the activities they have been doing. Explain that you need a shortened version to show as many different activities as possible. Whether they choose to speak or not will depend on their confidence in performing for an audience, but the choice is theirs. This prevents any undue pressure on those who are shy at performing, without restricting the more confident children. Explain that after the performance, the audience will be asked to guess what activities were enjoyed by these visitors. Use the words *Action* and *Freeze* to start and stop the drama as before. Keep this fairly short. It needs to be long enough for the performers to demonstrate a few activities but stop if children appear to be repeating activities, are unsure what to do next or if some are taking the performance into a long improvisation.
- It helps if the audience are asked to guess what activities they witnessed rather than which children carried them out. This avoids the possibility that some children will not be

84 *Drama as a Compelling Context*

mentioned and helps prevent any negative comments about individuals. You can mention any missed activities yourself if necessary.
- Praise the actors for their clear and imaginative miming and the audience for their concentration and observations.
- Then ask the audience to take their turn to perform their actions, with the other half guessing in the same way.

Reflection

- Ask the children if they enjoyed their visit to Sunny Park when they were the visitors. What was the most popular activity and were there any problems? Could anything be improved? Ask them to pick out their own favourite activity and share it with their group.

Writing in the classroom

- The children's experience of dramatic play provides the basis for some persuasive and descriptive writing for the Visitors Centre bookshop. This can be in the form of an information leaflet, weblog, story, poem or playscript entitled *A Day at Sunny Park*. It could also take the form of a review or recommendation for Sunny Park.
- The writing can also be illustrated based on their experiences in the drama. This can take the form of artwork for sale in the shop with a few descriptive sentences written underneath.

Drama in the hall

- Recreate Sunny Park in the hall along with the map and ask the children to sit in their groups along with you in the Visitors Centre.
- Ask them if they will now play the parts of the people who work in and look after Sunny Park. Ask them if they can accept that you could play the part of the manager or supervisor when wearing a particular scarf or other sign of role.
- Explain that the drama will start before the visitors arrive when the workers are checking the attractions and preparing them. Talk about some of the jobs they will need to do such as making sure the play equipment is safe, repairing the bridge and boundaries, feeding animals, securing boats, making food for the café, etc.
- Then allow groups a short time to decide what jobs they will need to do to look after their particular attraction when the drama starts and think about how they might mime them.
- Explain that you will start the drama with a narration describing the workers arriving to complete their jobs. Groups should stand up and walk into the space to start their jobs when you point to them. Start the teacher narration as follows: *It was early in the morning when the workers began to arrive to carry out their jobs at Sunny Park. These* (point to a few groups) *were the first to arrive... followed by these workers* (point to the other groups) *until everyone was busy working.*
- Put on the scarf to take on the role of manager and visit each group to ask how their jobs are going and if there are any problems.

An imaginary community: Key stage one and lower key stage two 85

- Stop the drama on the word *Freeze* and take off the scarf. Then resume teacher narration, to tell them that the manager has called the workers to an important meeting in the Visitors Centre. When you say the word *Action* you will put on your scarf to play the manager and wait for them in the Visitors Centre.

PART B: SOLVING PROBLEMS
Once children become engaged with the context, you can introduce one or more problems for them to solve which can provide opportunities for writing. The choice of problem is flexible and should be chosen to suit your learning objectives and the needs of the children. You can use either or both of the following examples or use them as a guide to make up your own.

Problem One: The storm

- Sit by the map so everyone can see it. At the meeting, tell the children that a bad storm is expected tonight with rain that could swell and flood the river and winds that could cause damage to buildings and other attractions. Ask the workers what kind of damage the storm might do to Sunny Park and what they could do to make it safer. You may need to make a few suggestions like tying up boats or swings, moving things away from the river if possible, etc. The nature of the preparations will depend on the attractions but those whose attractions would not be affected can check any communal areas such as the bridges and the Visitors Centre.
- Allow groups time to decide what they will do to make Sunny Park as safe as possible during a storm and when they are ready they can begin the jobs. Walk around in role as the manager to make suggestions and ask workers what they have done so far, etc. Then go round and ask them to join you in the Visitors Centre to report back.
- Once back in the Visitors Centre, ask each group to report back on what they have done.
- Take off the scarf to come out of role and pause the drama using the words: *Freeze. I'm stopping the drama for a minute to tell you what happened next. That night there was a terrible storm. Heavy rain fell all night and many rivers around the country were flooded. High winds blew down trees and ripped the roofs off some houses. When the workers arrived at Sunny Park the next morning they were worried about what damage they might find. When I say the word* Action, *we're moving time on to the morning after the storm when the workers met the manager in the Visitors' Centre.*
- Put on your scarf to resume the role of manager and restart the drama on the word *Action*. In role as the manager, comment on how bad the storm was last night and ask if any workers had damage done to their house. Then ask the workers to go to their attractions to see what damage has been done. They can take photos of the damage on their phones if they wish. Ask them to take just a quick look and then meet back in the Visitors Centre to report the damage and prepare a plan of what to do.
- Call the workers back after a short while and ask each group to report what damage they have seen. Talk about and plan what can be done and then ask the workers to carry out the plan. Some may work on communal areas like the boundary if they have attractions that would not be affected.

- Visit each group to check on progress and then call another meeting in the Visitors Centre. You can pause the drama to move time on to the meeting and restart it again.
- Praise the workers for everything they have done. Suggest that the workers need to write down everything they did to remind them in case there is another storm. It may also make an interesting information booklet for the bookshop. Stress that, due to their hard work, it is now safe to open Sunny Park for visitors again.
- Take off the scarf to come out of role and stop the drama on the word *Freeze*.

Reflection

- Talk about storm damage to real parks and beautiful places and how they can be made safe for visitors. Ask how many pretended to take photos of the damage and suggest they draw the imaginary photos back in the classroom, as these would be good for the information booklet.

Writing in the classroom

- Ask each child or group to draw the damage they saw in the drama and write a short sentence or paragraph about what they did as workers. Collect this into a booklet for the Sunny Park shop.
- Children can also design and make other small items for the shop which include written elements such as bookmarks with information about the park, greeting cards with pictures and a sentence about the park and any other items the children may suggest.

Problem Two: A complaint about litter

Drama in the hall

- In role as the manager tell the workers that you have had a letter from someone who visits Sunny Park. Either compose a letter to read out or tell the workers what the letter says. The letter writer loves the park and walks with their dog every day but is not coming back anymore because there is too much litter and rubbish. The dog cut its paw on a broken bottle in the woods and had to go to the vets. The person complains that there are no bins or not enough bins and no signs up about litter. Alternatively, you can take on the role of this person by asking the children to accept you as a visitor who has come with a complaint and use teacher-in-role to provide the same information. If you choose to use teacher-in-role then leave the workers to solve the problem rather than engage in a lengthy conversation as the children need time to consider the solutions.
- Discuss the issue by asking the following kinds of questions:
  - *Do we need to do anything about the litter? Why? What damage can it do?*
  - *What kind of bins do we need? Do we want bins that are bright and colourful so people will see them easily or will that spoil the beauty of the park? Do we want bins that fit in with the natural colours of the park like brown, green or camouflaged or will that mean people won't notice them?*
  - *Where shall we put the bins? What is the best place? How often will we empty them?*

An imaginary community: Key stage one and lower key stage two 87

- o Do we need signs telling visitors not to drop litter or to put their litter in bins? What will the signs say? Do we want to tell visitors not to drop litter or do we need to be more polite and ask them? Do we need signs to explain what damage litter can do to wildlife and animals?

- Staying in role, explain that it will take some time to design the bins and write the signs but for now, the workers need to tidy up any litter. Ask them to find bin bags in the sheds around the park and gloves to pick up any litter. They should put the full bags behind the Visitors Centre for the next rubbish collection. Ask them to notice any places where there is a lot of litter because that is where they need the bins.
- Let the workers pick up the litter and join in as you see fit. Then ask them to return to the Visitors Centre to report back on the kind and location of any litter they have found. Praise them for their work and tell them their next job is to design the bins and write the signs. Then stop the drama using the word *Freeze*.

Reflection

- Ask the children if they think other parks have a problem with litter and what they do about it. Have they noticed any signs or bins around parks they may have visited? If so what were they like? Were there any signs and if so what did they say?

In the classroom

- Children design bins and write appropriate signs for Sunny Park. These can be displayed in the shop area as examples of what is happening to keep the place clean.
- Work with the class to write a reply to the person who complained about the litter and then send the workers a reply the next day thanking them for their work. The person promises to return to Sunny Park to walk her dog like before.

Extension activities

- Link to books dealing with the problem of litter in public places such as **STELLA AND THE SEAGULL** by Georgina Stevens, **CATS' EYE VIEW OF ... LITTER** by O. Lonergan and **DINOSAURS AND ALL THAT RUBBISH** by Michael Foreman.
- Look at/research other parks and compare and contrast them to Sunny Park via a list of attractions.

8 An imaginary community
Upper key stage two

Contents	
Upper key stage two example 1: A village under threat	89
Upper key stage two example 2: A historical community	96
Mantle of the expert	100

Drama strategies

Freeze-frames
Improvisations
Meet and Greet
Pathway
Spotlighting
Teacher-in-role
Whole group drama

Overview

An imaginary community is an extremely flexible strategy that can accommodate a wide range of contexts for learning, including writing. The term community encompasses a wide range of contexts, including groups of residents in a street, a block of flats, a village, a town, an island, a castle or a city suburb. It can also include employees in a factory or in the tourist industry and groups with a common interest such as children who have created a secret club or play area.

The drama can be based on a community in a story, such as the community of Eerie-on-Sea in **MALAMANDER by Thomas Taylor,** or on inhabitants reflecting a particular historical period such as a Viking settlement or a seaside village in Victorian times.

The community itself can be developed from a basic given outline or created entirely by the children. Most contexts have the potential to provide a range of opportunities for writing but what tends to motivate the writing is not so much the context, as the sense of ownership and belonging created by the ongoing drama. A strong sense of ownership will accommodate pauses in the drama for the children to complete relevant writing tasks. In an ongoing drama about an imaginary community, it is the drama rather than the teacher that drives the need to write.

DOI: 10.4324/9781003315742-11

UPPER KEY STAGE TWO EXAMPLE 1: A VILLAGE UNDER THREAT

Opportunities for writing

Write a historical narrative and a poem or song for a particular purpose and audience.
Design an advertisement/poster making use of appropriate linguistic and other typical text features.
Write a character study.
Produce descriptive and persuasive writing.
Write a short playscript.
Write a non-chronological report in the form of a letter or news item.
Devise either an appropriate presentation or suitable questions to promote discussion.

Planning and resources

- Select a suitable problem for the village that reflects a learning area you wish to focus on.
- Decide on the best options in Section A for your writing objectives.
- Choose an appropriate name for the village, an approximate location and a distinguishing feature such as an ancient oak tree, a stately home or a monument.
- Decide on a method for 'publishing' the writing. This can be via some kind of classroom display about the village, a booklet or an online publication. This will be added to as the narrative of the drama progresses.

You will need

- A basic plan of the village with the distinguishing feature, a community centre and a few essential services such as a primary school, shops, health centre, etc.;
- Appropriate resources to enable the writing to be published;
- (Part A Option i) Role cards if appropriate;
- (Part A Option ii) Space to create a whole class freeze-frame.

Section A: WRITING TO BUILD BELIEF

This section aims to build belief in the village and develop a sense of ownership that will motivate the writing.

Building the belief is crucial to the success of both the drama and the writing. This example is designed to form a unit of work with pauses for writing lessons between the drama sessions, but it can be shortened if necessary.

The Contract

- Ask the children to take on the roles of adults living in an imaginary village for a forthcoming drama. Give the village an appropriate name.
- Show the children a basic plan of the village and reveal the kind of location and the features. Indicate a few different areas where most people live.

'Publishing' the writing

- Explain that any writing linked to the drama about the village will be published via your chosen method.

Options

You can use all or any of the following four options, but the more options you choose at this stage, the greater the motivation will be for the writing.

1. **Children create the community's history**
   Opportunities for writing: *concise writing for public information; narrative writing in paragraphs or chapters for a particular audience; persuasive texts.*
   - Working in groups of three, ask children to compile a list of 3-5 important imaginary historical events that might appear on a plaque on the wall of the community centre. Talk about the kind of events that appear on plaques like these, such as sporting achievements, natural disasters, erection of key buildings or significant features of the village, etc. It's also helpful if the children are given some parameters regarding dates.
   - Ask each group to select one event from their list and write it as a short concise statement appropriate for a plaque, along with the date e.g. *1992 The 'x' village football team won the area cup; 1920 A memorial is erected on 'x' street to commemorate those who died in the war.* It's important to create a sense of ownership at this stage, so accept all suggestions, as long as they fit with school values and are appropriate. Use this as an opportunity to discuss this kind of writing i.e. the need to be concise but clear enough for the general public to understand. Discuss and share examples of historical plaques as necessary. Record the sentences in date order as the children share them with you and the rest of the class, inviting the children to help you edit them as you go along.
   - Display the list as a village plaque in your chosen publication.
   - Ask groups to illustrate their sentence in the form of a freeze-frame depicting their chosen event, as if it were in a book about the history of the village.
   - Individual children then draft and submit a paragraph or chapter based on their chosen event for the village history book. Model the typical features of your chosen book before asking children to write theirs, whether that be a modern information book, village website or an ancient library book.

2. **Children create a celebratory community event**
   Opportunities for writing: *write an advertisement, poster, song, poem or motto, making use of appropriate linguistic and other typical text features.*
   - Make a class freeze-frame depicting a photo of a community village event such as a parade, carnival or historical anniversary for the front of the brochure/website. Discuss the kind of things people would be doing at the event that would present a positive picture of the village. Then ask children to work in pairs to select and prepare a frozen depiction of themselves taking part. Build the freeze-frame up a few groups at a time and take the imaginary photo with the words *1,2,3... Freeze.*

An imaginary community: Upper key stage two 91

Children then use this as a stimulus for designing a poster or website link to advertise the event.
- Children make small group freeze-frames of other current attractions in the village and write about them for the website or in a brochure.
- Children compose a village song, poems and/or short plays to be performed at the event and/or a motto and heraldic shield for the village. The song, poems and plays can be performed, written out and added to your chosen village publication, along with any motto or shield.

3 **Children create/develop their individual roles**
Opportunities for writing: *pen portraits or character studies; viewpoints.*
- Children are either given basic role cards or asked to create their own roles as inhabitants of the village. Either of these can be used as a basis for writing a pen portrait or character study/description for a Who's Who of the village inhabitants. It may be worth pointing out that a character study or pen portrait is not to be confused with characterisation which is more applicable when writing a narrative.
- Most primary children gain greater benefit from creating their own roles within a given framework of questions such as Name; Occupation; Area of the village they live in; How long they have lived there; How they feel about living in the village. However, there are some occasions when role cards are the better option. If the forthcoming problem or issue relies on the inhabitants having a variety of different viewpoints about the village, then role cards can ensure a range of different perspectives. In addition, some older key stage two children enjoy the challenge of taking on and developing a given role. The decision whether or not to use role cards depends on the needs of the children, the learning objectives in terms of the forthcoming problem for the drama and the time available to create the role cards. Having said that, the cards will be a useful resource for other classes of children in the future.
- Role Cards: If you decide to use role cards, the information on the cards needs to be clear and accessible without being too specific. Providing general information without naming the person or the village means they can be used again as a resource with other classes and in different contexts. The role cards may or may not imply a range of different viewpoints about the village, but they do need to be vague enough for children to add more details of their own making. You can make simple or more complex versions of the role cards to suit the needs of the children. When working with role cards it's helpful if children work in pairs. They should read them to each other to ensure they understand them. The exact details on the role cards will depend on the nature of the village and your intended issue in the drama, but the following examples show how the information might be set out:
  1 *You are 40 years old and run a popular guesthouse in the village. Your visitors love the village and so do you. You bought the guesthouse 10 years ago and have many friends in the village.*
  2 *You are 50 years old, married with two teenage children and you own one of the village shops. You are a good business person but the shop is not attracting enough customers and you are not making enough money. Your children say the*

village is boring with not enough to do for young people. If things don't improve, you will sell the shop and move your family out of the village.

3   You are 19 years old and live with your mum and younger brother and sister in the village. You have just left college where you gained top marks in your exams. You are now looking for a job but there is no work in the village. Your mum is ill and you don't want to move away from home to find work.

4   You are 45 years old and moved to the village 2 years ago, to start up a business selling organic vegetables. The business is doing well and you now have two large dogs whom you take on long walks around the village. You love the village and would not want to move back to the city.

5   You are 32 years old and live in the village with your 7-year-old son and two cats. You work in one of the village shops but the shop owner says it might have to close due to too few customers. Your son loves the local school so you don't want to leave but you are worried that you won't find another job in the village if the shop closes.

6   You are a 60-year-old retired police officer who solved many famous crimes. You moved to the village a few years ago to enjoy the peaceful surroundings. You are interested in the history of the village and have plans to write a book about it.

7   You are 25 years old and you work as a vet's assistant in a nearby town. You have a small house in the village but you like it because you have a large garden where you keep lots of rescued pets. You would love to open an animal sanctuary in the village.

8   You are 35 years old and used to be an athlete but moved to the village when you became injured. You now work from home, helping to organise athletic events for charity. You help to organise sports events in the village and in the village school.

o   Whether you use role cards or ask children to create their own roles, they will need a model or a framework to help them write a pen portrait or character study for the Who's Who publication.

o   Once the children have written their character studies, you can organise a Meet and Greet drama activity where pairs walk around the room introducing themselves to other pairs in role. This activity needs to last long enough for most pairs to share their information a couple of times. After the activity, the children are asked what they can recall about the characters who live in the village.

o   The character studies can then be added to the Who's Who publication for the village, along with a thumbnail sketch of each person.

4   **Children describe their houses**

Opportunities for writing: *descriptive writing; persuasive writing.*

o   Children are asked to play the roles of everyday adult people in the community. Each child or small group is allocated an area of the village to live in. You can allow the children to choose their own areas, but if it would be problematic for all of them to select the same part of the village, you would need to allocate the areas to ensure a more equal distribution.

An imaginary community: Upper key stage two 93

- Make sure the children understand that they will all be playing the parts of adults. This ensures they play roles able to make decisions and respond with responsibility later in the drama.
- Ask each child to sketch the front of their house and/or a view from one of their windows.
- Then ask each child to think of one distinctive thing a visitor to the village might notice when passing their house. Offer a few examples such as something the visitor might see or sense like the sound of a dog barking, a gate creaking, a football bouncing against a wall, someone on a trampoline or the smell of baking or flowers, etc.
- Use The Pathway drama strategy, where the children form two lines in a semicircle to represent their houses and the teacher-in-role as the visitor walks past them. Alternatively, children can remain seated as the visitor walks past, using the desks to represent the houses. Each child describes out loud what this visitor might notice as they pass by their house. It helps if the visitor repeats what each child says, to add status to their contribution and ensure everyone else keeps focused.
- Then ask the children to use this information and invent other details to write a paragraph for the estate agent's description of their house when it was last for sale. They can use the sketch they made of their house to support the information but may want to adapt it to make it appear more attractive. Use this to point out the role of illustrations and photos in a persuasive text. Offer models of estate agents' persuasive writing to support the work as appropriate.

Section B: WRITING TO SOLVE A PROBLEM/ISSUE

Opportunities for writing

Writing from different viewpoints; devising formal questions and non-chronological reports.

This section presents the children with a problem designed to deepen their thinking around a particular issue and create further opportunities for writing.

The problem in the context of a village can centre around conflicts of interest relating to the development of land or other changes affecting the quality of village life and its culture or history. It could also include issues around a newcomer to the village or dealing with the threat or impact of a natural disaster or a man-made event such as the building of a high-speed rail link through the village.

This particular example relates to the issue of appropriate development of land within the village. It relates to the proposed selling of land near the village for a theme park. In this example, the land for sale is a stately home called Oakton Hall in the village of Oakton.

1 **Children temporarily take on a different role**
    - Ask the children to take on a very different role for the next part of the drama. Explain that they will return to their original roles later but for this part of the drama they must try to forget their roles as villagers. It can be helpful to present this as a challenge. Ask them to take on the roles of managers of R.C. Construction Company who make equipment for play areas and theme parks. The managers have been

called to an important meeting with the director. The company has been looking for a new site to build a theme park and the managers are hoping this will be the news they have been waiting for.
- Invite the children to rearrange the room slightly to reflect how the chairs and tables might be set for the meeting. Changing the setting helps to prepare the children for the change in the drama and gives them some ownership.
- Ask the children if they could accept you in role as the director during the drama when wearing a particular jacket or scarf.
- The purpose of the role of the director is to present the problem and give children an opportunity to speculate on the outcomes. As this is an authority role, it is important not to slip back into teacher mode. Talk to the children in a professional manner as if you were talking to the managers. Consider all their suggestions in a polite manner with appropriate challenges or questions.
- Put on the clothing as a sign of role and use the words *Action* and *Freeze* to start and stop the drama. In role as the director of R.C. Construction Company, welcome the managers to this important meeting. Give information about the possibility of a new site for the long-awaited theme park. Whilst the land has not yet been put up for sale, you have information from someone close to the person selling the land that it will be. You suggest that the company needs to act fast to secure such a good site to discuss plans to make an offer on a stately home and grounds called Oakton Hall to build a theme park. Despite the fact that some villagers may welcome more work and more tourists to the village, you suspect that the villagers may have objections, especially as you may offer to buy some houses to make a wider road through the village for access. Ask the managers to help you make a list of possible objections and ask them to suggest how the company might respond to these objections. Ask them to prepare for negative press coverage as you have heard that rumours are already going around the village.
- Take off your sign of role and stop the drama.

2 **Villagers respond to the problem**
- Before taking on the villager roles again, ask the children to spend a few minutes in silence thinking about how their role as a villager might respond to the rumours about the theme park. They are asked to think about what they will tell their fellow villagers about their feelings on this matter.
- Set the scene for the next part of the drama at a coffee morning in the village hall, where villagers are talking around tables in groups of 3–5. Use desks in the classroom and seat pupils in mixed-ability groups for this.
- On the word *Action*, ask the children to take on their villager roles and talk in groups using spontaneous improvisation. They should ask each person in turn what they think to ensure all have an opportunity to speak. They should freeze when everyone in their group has spoken. This should last only a few minutes. Then stop the drama.
- Give groups time to develop these spontaneous improvisations into 1-minute polished improvisations, where they plan what each person will say beforehand.
- Invite groups or individuals to write their polished improvisations as short play scripts to be performed or collected into a booklet of short plays for the class.

An imaginary community: Upper key stage two 95

3 **Children find more information from a character**
Suggest that in the next part of the drama, the villagers should talk to the owner of the stately home to find out more information. In this example, the owner is a widow named Lady Harris.
- **Either** the villagers visit the stately home to talk to you as teacher-in-role as Lady Harris;
- **Or** they write a letter to Lady Harris with questions and you send a reply.
- The story in this example is that Lady Harris is keen to sell because her husband was the family heir and she has no connections and the hall is very expensive to run. She takes on board some of their concerns about a theme park but thinks that it may be good for the village in some ways. However, she will sell to the highest bidder no matter who they are.

4 **Villagers meet before writing letters**
- Villagers meet to discuss their response and write individual letters to the local newspaper or website to express their points of view.

5 **The Construction Company meets the villagers and the press**
Children work in three groups for this part of the drama. Two groups will be asked to play different parts during the drama so it is best to ask for volunteers.
- Ask for volunteers to temporarily play the roles as a small group of representatives from R.C. Construction Company who have agreed to meet the villagers and the press at the community centre to discuss the prospective theme park. They will be given time to write a presentation on the advantages of a theme park to the village.
- Ask for volunteers to play the roles of a small group of journalists who will ask questions during the proceedings. The journalists are from four different newspapers or organisations and will be given time to prepare and write questions to ask the villagers and the construction company.
- A third group remains as the villagers who work in pairs to write questions for the construction company.
- Ask the children to accept you as the neutral chairperson when sitting in a particular chair. Explain that the meeting will be recorded for local TV or social media.
- When groups have finished their written preparations, ask the children to arrange the room for a meeting. Let the children decide which groups sit where.
- Using the words *Action* and *Freeze* to stop and start the drama, ask everyone to sit in their places and then chair the meeting so everyone has their say. Children are usually sensible with their disagreements, but if anyone should behave inappropriately then try to deal with it in role as the chair. If this doesn't work, stop the drama and deal with the problem before restarting.

6 **Children write reports from different perspectives on the same event**
- The journalists write their press reports.
- The construction company writes reports for their director.
- The villagers write their version of events in a diary or for the website/social network or the local paper.

7 **Concluding the problem**
- The drama can end here with a letter from Lady Harris on her decision to sell the land to the National Trust or a letter from the construction company telling the villagers that they have found more appropriate land away from the village but nearby.

If the children have suggested another feasible solution then you can use that idea as the conclusion.

Section C: REFLECTION

Remind the children that this has been imaginary and ask them to comment on whether there are any similar situations in real life. Invite them to look at real-life theme park literature, websites, etc. for locations and standards of writing, etc., and/or look at letters/articles on real environmental issues such as location of wind farms, etc.

Celebrate all the writing that has occurred as a result of the drama. Ask the children to comment on the difference between writing as themselves and writing in role after experiencing the role in the drama.

Extension activities

- Write a diary/letter to a friend on key events in role as a villager.
- Children write about what they would feel if they really lived there and were not in role.
- Write about the experience of being in the drama and what they think they have learnt.

UPPER KEY STAGE TWO EXAMPLE 2: A HISTORICAL COMMUNITY

The drama can take the form of a historical community reflecting a particular period in time and place. This can be people living in a settlement, itinerant groups or servants living in a castle or a big house. Children can check for historical accuracy before and/or after the drama by reading information books.

Planning and resources

Children need some basic background of the chosen historical period before taking part in the drama.

You will need

- A hall or cleared space and a few chairs for the drama work;
- A small whiteboard or sign for each group;
- Small items of clothing such as scarves or cloaks as a sign of teacher-in-role;
- Resources to make a class book;
- Examples of historical information books.

PART A: BUILDING BELIEF

In the classroom

The contract

- Ask the children if they will take part in a drama to play the parts of people living in your chosen historical period. They will be ordinary people living together in a community at the time.

An imaginary community: Upper key stage two   97

'Publishing' the writing

- Explain that the children will use the drama to help them write an information book - a fictionalised history book about their experiences for the class book corner.

Preparing the roles

- Organise the children into small groups and allocate each group an appropriate occupation for that community e.g. weavers, potters, archers, carpenters and farmers. If they are servants, they will need relevant jobs. Four to six occupations will suffice.
- Ask groups to help each other write some information about their characters including their names, ages, families, living conditions and the tasks they perform each day in the community. Groups can decide if they live together or are related or are just friends. Refer to information books or other resources as necessary. Make it clear that this writing is for an information book and should therefore be fairly factual in tone. Children can also add a sketch of their characters.
- Explain that the drama will start on an ordinary day in the community. Ask groups to decide on the jobs they will do first when the drama starts and how they might mime them. Make it clear that they will need to mime the actions but should talk as if they were really there when in the drama.
- Ask each group to write a sign showing their occupation in the hall during the drama, so others can locate them even though there probably wouldn't be a sign in some historical periods.

Drama in the hall

Defining the space

- Ask the children to sit together at one side of the hall and in their groups.
- Place chairs around three sides of the hall to represent each occupation. Place the signs on the chairs to indicate where each group works. Ask the children to accept that this could be where they live and that each chair represents the back of where groups live. Define any areas or equipment that are out of bounds for the drama.
- Explain that the drama will start with a freeze-frame of the moment everyone started their work. Provide some examples such as a carpenter might be just about to chop some wood with their hands raised. Ask groups to decide on how they will be positioned for the freeze-frame.
- Suggest that groups might exchange goods for things they need rather than using money e.g. a baker might offer a carpenter some bread in exchange for firewood. Mention one item that each group could use to exchange for something else, so the children have an idea of what to do.
- Ask the children if you can be in the drama in role as someone in the community who works alone but helps others. Choose a role that has something everyone will need so you can interact with all groups, such as a farmer bringing eggs or vegetables or an herbalist. Explain that you will play that role whenever you wear the scarf but if you are

not wearing the scarf then you are not in role. This enables you to move in and out of the drama as appropriate.
- Make it clear that you will start and stop the drama using the words *Action* and *Freeze*.
- Invite groups to take up their frozen positions a few at a time to ensure they understand the concept. When everyone is in place, use the words *Freeze. Hold still. When I say Action, this place will come to life. Action.*

Dramatic play

- As children come to life, visit each group in turn to build belief in the drama. If children are not used to drama they may be embarrassed at first so don't insist on a response. Try to use slightly formalised language suited to the times and speak with sincerity as a model of how to play a role. Most children cope with this kind of dramatic play, but if a few children are having problems that disrupt the others, take off the scarf to come out of role and have a quiet word to remind them of the contract or ask them to observe until they feel they can join in.
- Let this run for as long as children are engaged or until most groups have completed their jobs. Then stop the drama with the word *Freeze* and ask groups to return to sit in front of their signs.
- Ask half the groups to recreate their original freeze-frame starter and on the word *Action*, they should show the other groups the kind of jobs they were doing. Those watching should try to guess the jobs rather than the children who performed them. Keep this fairly short and make sure children do not criticise each other's performances. Then repeat with the other groups. This gives status to the jobs and allows them to share their work.

Reflection

- Ask the children to comment on the following question: *We can never recreate history but according to what we know about this period of history how close were we to what it was really like?* Agree to check any details back in the classroom using the information books and resources available.

Writing in the classroom

- Based on their experiences in the drama, children can write a *Day in the Life of* their character for the class information book.

PART B: THE PROBLEM
Your choice of problem will be dependent on your chosen historical period e.g.

- Celts faced with the prospect of the Roman invasion must decide if they should fight or run.
- A small Victorian seaside town is having a railway – will it be a good or bad thing and how do they prepare?

An imaginary community: Upper key stage two 99

- The castle may be attacked or put under siege, what can the residents do to prepare?
  The problem can be communicated via a letter or an announcement from yourself as teacher-in-role or you can narrate the problem.
- Recreate the drama for a short while before introducing the problem so children can get back into role. Then stop the drama and narrate that later that day the community met to solve an important problem. If you choose to play a different role to communicate the problem then explain that to the children beforehand and use a different form of clothing such as a draped cloak or a hat. Otherwise, introduce the problem via your original role on the word *Action*.
- If you have chosen to play a different role to introduce the problem then stop the drama and narrate that the person left. Then explain you will be returning to your original role for the rest of the meeting. This sounds confusing, but children will accept it as long as you explain the process and carry out the roles with confidence.
- If you have introduced the problem via your original role then keep this going for the rest of the meeting.
- Talk about some possible solutions to the problem before asking groups to go back to their homes and talk about what they think.
- Stop the drama and move time on to that evening when the groups were sitting together talking about the problem. Give children a minute to think about what their role might say before bringing the drama to life. This means everyone is talking but there is no audience. Remind groups to ask every person what they think.
- Use the **Spotlighting** drama strategy to listen in to the improvised conversations. To do this, stop the drama after a short while with the word *Freeze* and explain that your original role was curious and that night they walked around the homes listening in to snippets of conversations. Explain that groups will come alive and carry on their conversations when you walk up to them and stop to listen. When you move away they should stop. Allow each group a short time only and try to stop on an interesting comment or point. It may be useful to comment aloud to summarise what you have heard e.g. *some of the potters think we should fight the Romans but the others are too afraid. I wonder what the weavers are saying.*
- Finally, call another meeting to discuss the problem and decide what to do.
- Stop the drama and narrate what happened next. Use drama to re-enact the solution if possible e.g. use dramatic play to prepare the castle for siege or create a freeze-frame of the first conflict with the Romans or arrange for the community to meet another role to obtain more information. If it's not possible to re-enact the solution then narrate what happened next and conclude with a freeze-frame.

Consequences of decisions

- If appropriate you can challenge and extend children's knowledge and understanding of what the consequences of their solutions might be, either via teacher-in-role offering information or via a narration of what happened as a result of their decisions. You can also replay the decisions to see what might happen if the community made a different decision. This is an example of where drama can provide what Dorothy Heathcote once called a 'No Penalty Zone' where children can try again without penalty.

Reflection

- Ask the children if they think the problem in the drama was something that historical communities really had to deal with and ask them to check information books and resources back in the classroom.
- Ask the children if imagining they were people in history helped them understand more what it might have been like and what problems communities were faced with. Compare the experience to reading a historical novel written from the point of view of a character such as books by **Emma Carroll** and **Lesley Parr**.
- Link the problem to similar problems in the present day if appropriate.

Mantle of the expert

Mantle of the expert was a term used by drama pioneer Dorothy Heathcote to describe a drama strategy where expertise is draped metaphorically upon the shoulders of the children like a mantle. This can happen in small ways when a teacher plays a role that knows less than the children about a topic or class novel or when children receive an imaginary letter asking for advice. There are many examples of this approach in this book. However, Mantle of the Expert can be applied as a cross-curricular project to provide an effective means to engage children in learning, including opportunities for writing. When used in this way, children are asked to take on the roles and responsibilities of an imaginary community of experts that have been contacted by a client requesting their help or information. This can be delivered via teacher-in-role, written or by other means. Children then move out of the fiction to learn the necessary skills and knowledge and work in teams to undertake the task or assignment. When the task is concluded, the children return to the fiction to consider the impact. Children can take on expert roles like designers, historians, archaeologists, editors, environmentalists, film-makers, directors, etc. Some schools use this as a whole-school approach to learning which is very effective. The drama provides the imaginary context which drives purposeful learning and will include opportunities for writing reports and other forms of writing. There may or may not be further drama input until the end of the task.

There is an excellent website with ideas and resources dedicated to this approach at mantleoftheexpert.com and more details are available in ***A BEGINNER'S GUIDE TO MANTLE OF THE EXPERT* by Tim Taylor.** See also ***DRAMA FOR LEARNING* by Dorothy Heathcote and Gavin Bolton.**

9 An imaginary journey

Opportunities for writing

Lists, diaries, logs, reports and fact finders.

Contents	
Key stage one examples	102
Key stage two example: The expedition	105

Drama strategies

Freeze-frames
Teacher-in-role and/or teacher as narrator
Whole-group drama

Overview

An imaginary journey is a very flexible whole-group drama scenario that provides a number of opportunities for writing. The means of travel and the destination and purpose of the journey offer a multitude of variations on the same outline structure. Journeys can be taken on foot and/or by bus, train, plane, ship, raft, hot-air balloon, spaceship, magic carpet, on horseback or via a time machine. The possibilities are endless. The same goes for the destination and purpose. Travellers can take a journey to somewhere in the past, present or future, either real or imagined. The journey can be a complete fantasy or a real world with a fantasy element. The travellers can set off to explore a new land, rescue someone, complete a challenge for a charity, escape from something or someone, obtain something for a good cause or discover the answer to a mystery, etc. They can stand as imaginary events or be linked to events and characters in stories. Whatever the reason for the journey, there needs to be a problem to solve at some point in order to deepen the experience. The problem can be an obstacle to overcome or an issue to solve. The opportunities for writing will vary according to the events, but all journeys require preparation, including lists of what to take, and an opportunity to reflect on and record the experience via a diary, log or report. Some journeys may also attract the interest of the local news or national media.

DOI: 10.4324/9781003315742-12

102   *Drama as a Compelling Context*

KEY STAGE ONE EXAMPLES

Most journeys at key stage one are designed to last for one drama lesson in a hall followed by writing in the classroom.

Planning and resources

- Decide on the reason for your journey, the destination, the means of getting there and a problem for the children to solve. This can be linked to a topic or a well-known story. With younger children, the problem can be as simple as how to cross a river with a broken bridge or help a character from a story.
  The following will provide a few ideas which can be adapted:
  1. *Journey on a spaceship to outer space to land on the moon. A bad landing means the ship has to be repaired. Walking on the moon with heavy boots makes it more difficult to carry out repairs. The astronauts take photos and then leave.*
  2. *Journey to Storyland on a bus. This is a gentle drama more suitable for the youngest children who feel more secure with familiar stories. It also represents a holding form that can be used many times allowing the travellers to become involved in a different story each time they visit Storyland. They may meet a story character (teacher-in-role) or discover a note from a character who needs help with some physical activity that has potential to be mimed in the drama e.g. the prince needs help to cut down the forest to rescue Sleeping Beauty, a cook needs help to make food for the wedding party of Cinderella or Snow White because the servants are ill or Santa's elves need help to make the toys in time for Christmas. Other characters from less traditional stories may also need help to carry out an activity, such as Dad and Lizzie who need help to repair the house in* **LIZZIE AND THE BIRDS by Dawn Robertson.**
  3. *Journey on a magic boat to Unicorn Island to find and take photos of unicorns. Children write a list of facts about unicorns before the journey to help find them. The Queen or King of Unicorn Island will not let them off the boat until they are reassured the children won't harm or scare the unicorns. The travellers are asked what they know about unicorns. Problems then occur in crossing the island to locate the unicorns that live beyond the caves in a magic forest. Children are sent in pairs to find the unicorns and take photos. Children must retrace their steps to get back to the boat.*
  4. *Journey on horseback or on a school bus to a country farm to see the animals. They write facts about the animals before setting off. The farmer is sick and needs help to feed and look after the animals. The children receive instructions from the farmer and then set to work.*
  5. *Journey in a time machine takes the children to Isaac Newton's farm where they go to explore. The children meet Isaac's mother or father who asks for help to pick the apples in the orchard. His/her son Isaac will not help today as he is busy writing about something important called gravity that she/he doesn't understand. She/he asks the children if they know what gravity is. They pick the apples and help with other jobs before returning to the time machine and the present day.*

You will need

- A hall or cleared space for the drama lesson(s);
- A scarf or apron as a sign of teacher-in-role.

What to do

In the classroom

- Ask the children if they will join you in pretending to go on a journey. Describe the means of transport and the destination and reason for taking the journey but do not mention the forthcoming problem. Explain that they will need to prepare for the journey. This may involve writing a fact-finding page if the journey involves creatures like unicorns or farm animals. Talk about what to take and then either write a list with the children or ask them to work in pairs to write their own lists.
- Ask them to pretend that all the things they are taking are near to them and within easy reach. Demonstrate packing your own things using mime before asking the children to do the same.
- Explain that you will be using the hall to go on the imaginary journey.

In the hall or cleared space

- Ask the children to sit together in pairs facing into the hall. If children have not had drama in the hall before, then define the space where the journey will take place. Use the words *Action* and *Freeze* to start and stop the action in the drama but start with a narration before you say *Action* e.g. *This is the story of some children and their teacher who went on a bus/train/spaceship/boat... to .... Action.*
- Describe the means of transport is in front of them by remarking on how good it looks. Ask the children if you can take their photo before they leave and either take a real photo or pretend to take one. Ask them how they are feeling about the journey.
- Organise the children to board the transport in pairs in an orderly manner as if on a school trip. Ask them to take their seats and put their bags somewhere safe.
- The next part will depend on the means of transport. If you are on a bus, you can sit at the front and talk to an imaginary bus driver who says they can sing if they like as long as it is not too loud. Then suggest a song and sing it to suggest the passing of time on the journey. If on a train, ship, magic carpet or hot-air balloon, then narrate what they can see from the windows, the deck or far below them. If on a spaceship, they will need to put on their space suits and strap themselves in before you do a countdown to lift off. Then narrate what they feel as the ship lifts off and finally announce they can undo their seat belts.
- The journey on the transport need not take long. It needs to be long enough to create the illusion of travel. When you are ready, announce that you have arrived at your destination on the transport and tell them what you can see at this point. This information sets the scene.
- Organise the children to disembark in a crocodile formation or similar so you can walk to a safe place to sit in a group to decide where to go next. This will depend on your choice

of journey. A journey to storyland where they will meet a character will usually mean they will follow you in a crocodile formation as you walk through a forest environment or similar. They may think they are just exploring the forest at this point. Other journeys mean they walk a short way before they are asked to go off in pairs to explore, take photos with their imaginary cameras and return with information.

Introducing the problem

- If the problem does not involve you taking on another role, such as crossing a river, then introduce the problem in role by telling the children what you can see ahead and ask them for suggestions on how to deal with the problem. If you need to take on another role such as a character then stop the drama and tell the children that you will now tell them what happened next. Then narrate what they saw or met or what happened. Ask them to pretend that you could be the character when you put on the scarf. Explain to younger children that you will come back to being yourself later on. If you are playing a well-known character then try not to use a voice or mannerisms that are too extreme as young children can find this disturbing or distracting. Integrity is the key so try to keep in role as long as you need to, then take off the scarf to come out of role.

Solving the problem

- Whether this is in role as a character or as the teacher, ask the children for suggestions on how to solve the problem. They may need to talk in pairs first if appropriate. Talk through every idea and try to use as many as possible. This usually takes the form of some kind of dramatic play where children mime actions such as repairing the spaceship, working out how to climb a mountain or through a cave or making food for a party, etc.

Retracing steps

- Once the problem is solved then praise the children and ask if they can remember how to get back to the transport. Then retrace the journey but quicker than when you came. If it would take too long then narrate all or part of the journey back. Finally, board the transport and narrate the journey home.
- Stop the drama with the words *Freeze and that is the end of our story.*
- Ask the children which parts of the story they liked best and talk about how well they solved the problem.

In the classroom

- Ask children to write a few sentences and draw a picture to describe what they saw when they went exploring.
- Ask more confident writers to write about all or part of their journey to tell others what happened. This can be in the form or a story map and/or diary or letter to a friend. Talk about the beginning, middle and end of the story and what happened in each part.

An imaginary journey 105

- Display the work alongside the photo taken at the outset or ask the children to sketch a small image of themselves in the photo if you took an imaginary one.

Extension activities

- Children prepare a presentation about their journey for an assembly or for another class. The writing can be part of this presentation with children giving verbal accounts of how they solved the problem along with a freeze-frame or frames to illustrate key moments.
- Children write a class poem from the point of view of someone or a creature they met on the journey such as a unicorn when it first saw the travellers. What did it think and feel? Was it scared or curious, etc.?

KEY STAGE TWO EXAMPLE: THE EXPEDITION

Whilst a journey for key stage two children can easily take place in one drama lesson with a follow-up writing lesson, the children gain more opportunities for writing when the journey is spread out to incorporate at least two drama lessons. The journey then becomes more of an expedition with opportunities for children to engage with more problems and challenges which have the potential to create a need for some kind of written response. Journeys can be similar to fictional or real-life expeditions as an introduction to a novel or non-fiction book featuring a journey or they can be invented by the children themselves as an adventure with problems arising in an open-ended fashion or set by the teacher. Some journeys can be set in the context of a charity game show made up of challenges set by the children themselves or by groups for each other. Some journeys like space journeys can touch on the sci-fi genre whilst others can be more magical or realistic with a surprise fantasy or sci-fi twist. The possibilities are numerous but the journey usually follows a set framework as set out in the following example.

Planning and resources

- Decide what kind of expedition best suits the needs of the children, your learning objectives and your own confidence in using drama. Open-ended drama work requires knowledge of a range of drama strategies in order to respond appropriately. However, if you time it so the drama lesson ends with stating the problem, you will have time to select an appropriate drama strategy before the next drama lesson. Classes with poor social health or little experience in drama can manage open-ended work but they may respond better via some of the more structured drama strategies.
- Children will fill out logs as the expedition progresses so they need to make and design their own logbooks in advance or you can provide them if funds allow. A personal logbook makes the experience feel more authentic and engaging.

- Decide how many drama lessons and classroom writing lessons will meet your needs and plan the content accordingly.
- Either decide on a problem or problems the travellers will encounter or try to anticipate the kinds of problems that could occur if you are relying on the children's ideas.

You will need

- A hall or cleared space for the drama lessons;
- Scarves or similar small items of clothing for teacher-in-role as the need arises;
- Reference books or stories about similar journeys if appropriate.

What to do

In the classroom

- Ask the children if they will join you in creating a drama about an expedition. Provide them with information about the type of expedition, the reason for going and the destination. Explain that this will take place in the hall over a period of time, so the children can write logbooks in between the drama lessons as if they were explorers.
- Ask the children to design and make their own logbooks or create a cover for a ready-made one. Each child should write their name and the name of the expedition on their logbook.
- Talk about what equipment they will need to take and how they will transport it. Ask them to speculate about any problems they may encounter and whether they need any extra equipment for that. Individual children or groups may be given responsibility for certain items such as emergency food rations or the first aid kit, etc. Then ask individuals to list their personal equipment at the front of their logbooks with any diagrams or explanations, including any group equipment they are responsible for.
- Talk about what facts or other useful information they may need to know before setting off. Either ask the children to add this to the back of their logbooks for reference or produce a guide as a whole class.

Drama lesson 1: In the hall

The contract and dramatic play:

- If you plan for children to write in their logbooks during the drama, they will need to take them into the hall but explain that it will not be practical to carry them around during the drama. Children enjoy the authenticity of writing up the log as things happen in the drama, but it takes up more time in the hall, so the log can be written later if this is a problem.
- Ask the children to imagine that the hall is the setting for the expedition and mention any areas of the hall that are not in the drama. If the expedition involves transport to the setting then ask them to imagine it is there in the hall. Make it clear that everything they need will have to be mimed but when the drama starts they should talk as if they were really there. Ask for some examples of how actions can be mimed such as putting up a tent or stepping into a spaceship, etc.

An imaginary journey 107

- Introduce the words *Action* and *Freeze* to start and stop the drama.
- Suggest that the explorers would have a photo taken before they set off. Depending on the context, this could be for social media, the news or for relatives left behind. Ask the children to pose with their imaginary equipment as if they were setting out on the expedition. Take a real or imaginary photo before asking them how they are feeling about the expedition. This can be achieved as a freeze-frame where you touch some children on the shoulder to hear their thoughts.
- The next section will depend on your chosen means of travel. Use teacher narration to set the scene and lead into the drama e.g. *So the explorers set off on the expedition of a lifetime, carrying their equipment and wondering what they would find. Action!*
- If you are walking then organise the party in pairs before setting off. If you are boarding a means of transport such as a spaceship, plane, bus or ship, you will need to describe it and state where certain parts are located before boarding. You may also need to mime putting on relevant clothing such as space suits if necessary and do a countdown to lift off before the astronauts can loosen seat belts, etc. Narrate the journey on the transport by describing what the explorers might see as they travel. Then start the drama by saying *And this is what happened when the explorers arrived... Action*. Then immediately start to talk as if you were really there at this point.

Making camp

- Set off walking with the group as if you are one of the group. This is a different kind of teacher-in-role where you are there as one of the group, so you do not need to use a scarf as a sign of role or make a contract, as it is implied that you will take part. However, you will assume a kind of organiser role rather than a director so make suggestions rather than direct the proceedings.
- Mention what you can see around you as you walk but explain that it is late and you will need to find a good place to set up camp or find a sheltered place. Choose something appropriate to the context.
- Suggest a place to camp or shelter if the children do not suggest one as you walk and organise them into groups to set up tents or make a shelter. Ask them to join you by your tent or shelter when they have finished so you can plan what to do next.
- When most have camped, call everyone together. This next stage is flexible and will depend on what you intend in terms of the problems during the expedition. If you have a set problem you intend to introduce later then you may want to talk about the plans for the next day and then stop the drama. If you intend to use the children's ideas to formulate a problem or problems then you can ask pairs to spend a few minutes exploring the area around the camp to report back on what they see. You can then use what they have found to formulate a problem e.g. if they find mountains with fire then there could be a volcanic eruption pending or a dragon up there to combat. When children have reported back on their explorations verbally, then stop the drama.
- Explain that the explorers spent the evening filling in their logbooks to record the journey so far. Talk about what they might include.

In the classroom: Logbooks

- Talk about logbooks and how they are organised and how they appear, etc. and refer to any famous real-life examples of explorers' logbooks in sci-fi films or stories, etc.
- Ask children to fill in their own logbooks but allow them to work in pairs for support to remind them what happened.
- Ask pairs to choose a sentence from each of their logbooks to read to the rest of the class. Then compare experiences if appropriate.

Drama lesson 2: In the hall

The problem: This section will depend on your chosen context but will involve introducing the problem either via narration or via teacher-in-role giving information or a written document such as a letter, scroll or treasure map that has been discovered. It may also be some kind of mystery object or a mysterious message from aliens or a tribe, etc. This outline is a version with two drama lessons but more problems and open-ended work may involve more drama lessons.

- Start the drama where the group is packing up their camp and then maybe carry on the walking for a short while before introducing the problem.
- Allow the children to talk in pairs or threes before they make suggestions on how to solve the problem and take each suggestion seriously. There are rare occasions when a child, often new to drama work, will make a purposefully inappropriate suggestion. If you feel the suggestion is given as a challenge or to subvert the drama then try to take it at face value if you can, but if not then pause the drama and ask the child not to spoil the work in this way. Remind them that they agreed to imagine they were really there and ask if they wish to continue or observe. This is rare but having a plan for these kinds of situations will give you more confidence.

Useful drama strategies

When faced with children's solutions to problems, you can pause the drama to employ various drama strategies to depict what might or would happen.

- The simplest strategy is the **Freeze-frame** where children, either in groups or with one group at the front of the class, create a freeze-frame depicting or representing a solution, along with a caption. These can be brought to life for a short while before freezing again. Groups share their freeze-frames and the class vote on the one they want or think is most likely to happen.
- Another useful strategy is **Spotlighting** or overheard conversations where children talk about solutions in role in groups and the teacher then freezes the action and then unfreezes groups one at a time for a short while so everyone can hear what they are saying.
- **Hot-seating** is useful if the expedition encounters monsters or non-human forms as the teacher can sit on a chair to represent the voice of the creature as the children stand around or in front of the chair.

An imaginary journey 109

- **Teacher-in-role** is a powerful way to challenge solutions put forward by the children e.g. is the alien life force really going to attack the spaceship? An alien voice explains how they are just scared of what the explorers are doing on their planet.
- The children usually need to retrace their steps after solving the problem, in order to achieve a sense of completion but that may only need to be partly re-enacted. The means of transport they arrived in needs to be enacted but other parts can be narrated.

In the classroom

- Whether this be part of the drama lesson or narrated back in the classroom, some kind of final conclusion is required to form the final entry in the logbooks.
- If appropriate, the children can also write a news or media report of the expedition.

Reflection

- Talk about the different reasons why people go on expeditions and ask the children to think about how it might feel to go on this kind of journey. Consider universal questions such as: *Are expeditions just something for rich people to do? Should explorers take risks that may endanger emergency services? Is it fair to go on a dangerous expedition if you have a family to look after? Can expeditions lead to improvements in the world?*

Extension activities

- If appropriate, compare and contrast with expeditions in real life or fiction e.g. **SHACKLETON'S JOURNEY by William Grill** and **ARCTIC STAR by Tom Palmer** or stories like **COGHEART** and **SHADOWSEA by Peter Bunzel** and **SHIP OF SHADOWS by Maria Kuzniar.**
- Make a map of the expedition to display alongside the logbooks and media reports.
- Children prepare an assembly based on their expedition.

10 Open-ended drama

Opportunities for writing

Various according to the children's ideas, but includes creative writing and explanations.

Contents	
Key stage one examples	
a The letter	111
b The door	112
c The special box	113
d Dramatic play	114
Key stage two examples	
a The key	115
b Directing the story	116

Drama strategies

Teacher-in-role
Whole group drama
Other strategies as needed

Overview

Open-ended drama can be very exciting, especially when it leads to unexpected areas of cross-curricular learning. However, the main learning objective for open-ended drama in this chapter is to stimulate contexts and ideas for writing. The intention is to stimulate the start of a story, which develops according to the children's ideas to form a written story, poem or play. The drama can be used purely as a stimulus to create a story based on the children's initial ideas. In this case, the drama would be more of a helping hand for writing rather than a compelling context. However, developing the story through further drama work will provide a more compelling context for writing with further opportunities to write for other reasons before the final story. For example, if a character is in trouble the children may write some advice or if there is a problem to solve, they may write out their ideas for solutions to present to the group. Developing children's ideas through further drama is likely to be the best choice in terms of children's engagement and opportunities for writing. Children are likely to find the drama a more compelling context for writing if it is developed via an exploration of their own ideas.

However, the unpredictability of children's responses can be challenging if you have a limited fund of drama strategies to call on at a moment's notice. The choice of whether or not to develop the initial drama stimulus through further drama depends on your confidence in using a range of drama strategies without any pre-planning. Many experienced drama teachers find thinking on their feet in response to children's ideas to be the most challenging and yet the most rewarding and productive way of working.

The drama-in-education pioneer Dorothy Heathcote was an expert in this art.

(***DRAMA FOR LEARNING* by Dorothy Heathcote and Gavin Bolton and *DOROTHY HEATHCOTE: DRAMA AS A LEARNING MEDIUM* by Betty Jane Wagner**)

KEY STAGE ONE EXAMPLES

a   **THE LETTER**

Planning and resources

You will need

- A letter in an envelope addressed and with a stamp. The letter needs to have some writing on to make it look authentic but it won't actually be read by the children;
- A chair in a space at the front of the class;
- A board to record children's ideas;
- A scarf or small item of clothing as a sign of teacher-in-role.

What to do

- Place the letter in its envelope on the floor, a little way behind the chair as if it has come through a letter box.
- Ask the children to imagine that the chair is in someone's house where they are about to find a letter. Ask them if they can pretend that you are that person when wearing the scarf.
- Ask the children to watch what happens when the person opens the letter.
- Put on the scarf and sit on the chair. Talk aloud to yourself saying things like *Oh I think I heard the letter box. I wonder who can be sending me a letter today. It's not a special day like my birthday or anything so I wonder what it can be.*
- Walk to the letter, pick it up and carry it to your chair. Open the letter with a positive expression on your face, but as you read it your expression changes to looking sad and then you begin to mutter *Oh dear Oh dear*. Then pause before putting the letter away either in your pocket or under the chair and then take off the scarf to come out of role. Get up from the chair and move away from it. Make it clear that you are no longer pretending to be that person.

- Ask the children to tell a partner what they think the letter is about. Then ask for suggestions and write them up on a board where they can all see.
- Talk about which of these suggestions would make a good story and either move straight to writing the story plan or select an idea to explore further. This can be explored through a simple drama strategy such as a freeze-frame with a group at the front of the class e.g. if the idea is that the letter is from a sick relative then the freeze-frame can be of the moment when the person goes to visit them. This can present another opportunity for the children to draw the frozen moment and then write the speech and/or thought bubbles with a sentence underneath describing the event.
- Use this further exploration to plan a short story with the children which you can write together or ask children to write on their own. Confident children can use one of the other ideas to develop their own stories.

b THE DOOR

Planning and resources

You will need

- A space at the front of the class with two chairs placed apart to indicate where a large door is situated;
- A scarf or a similar item of clothing as a sign of teacher-in-role;
- A board to record children's ideas.

What to do

- Ask the children to pretend that the space between the two chairs is a very large door. Go up to the imaginary door and draw around the edge of it with your finger, indicating that it is too high to reach the top.
- Ask the children what they think might be behind such a large door. Collect a few ideas before writing some on the board.
- Tell them there is someone behind the door who would like to talk to them. Assure the children that this person is safe and will not harm them. Ask them who they think it might be. Select a person from these ideas that you think you could represent via teacher-in-role and ask the children if you can pretend to be that person when wearing the scarf. The person should have some kind of problem and needs advice from the children. If the children's ideas are not forthcoming or inappropriate then you can make up a person such as a giant who has no friends because everyone thinks they are scary when they are not. Or maybe the giant eats sweets all day but now has toothache and doesn't know what to do or why they have toothache. The giant needs advice on how to convince people they are friendly or how to prevent further toothache. Children then write to the people asking them to be kind to the giant or make a health poster for the giant about the importance of not eating too many sweets and cleaning your teeth.
- When the children have given their verbal advice in the drama, take off the scarf and announce that you are no longer that person.

- Depending on the children's ideas and the potential for development, you may want to explore what happened next. For example, you can use freeze-frames to depict the giant making friends or going to see the dentist.
- Talk about how to make this scenario into a written story and use the board to plan the events. Then either write the story with the class or ask the children to write their own story of what happened behind the door. Display the writing behind or within a door shape.

c **THE SPECIAL BOX**

Planning and resources

You will need

- A small box such as a shoe box with the words MY SPECIAL THINGS written on it;
- Three objects or two objects and one picture that can fit in the box. The objects are intended to be special to a character and need to have some potential for linking with each other. You can choose objects that indicate types of characters like pirates or magical creatures or you can choose objects with more general possibilities such as:
    a   a crown, an old key and a small toy pet or photo of a pet;
    b   a paintbrush, a pebble and a photo of a beach;
    c   a shell, a comb and a photo of a boat;
    d   a photo of a plane or spaceship, a child's birthday badge and a toy;
    e   a photo of a house, a dog's name tag and a small ball;
- Space at the front of the class or a cleared space for the drama work;
- A scarf as a sign of teacher-in-role if needed.

What to do

- Show the children the box and talk about how people keep special things. Make the distinction between a favourite thing and a special thing and talk about how a special thing for one person may not be special for others. Ask the children if any of them keep special things and invite them to share why those things might be special to them.
- Ask the children to pretend that this box of special things belongs to someone they don't know. Open the box and bring out the objects. Ask the children to guess what kind of person might own these objects and then talk about why they might have chosen these objects and why they might be special for them.
- Take one of the children's ideas about one or more of the objects and ask them to think about an event when the person obtained the object or when it was special e.g. the crown for when the queen was crowned; the child who painted a pebble on the beach that everyone loved; the child who saw a mermaid combing her hair beside a boat; the birthday treat to the moon; the child who lost his dog when throwing it a ball.
- Choose a group to come to the front of the class to make a freeze-frame of this moment based on the suggestions from the rest of the class. Talk about what the characters might be feeling and thinking if appropriate. Describe the moment and then do a countdown to

114 *Drama as a Compelling Context*

the freeze e.g. *this is the moment when ... became special. 1,2,3, Freeze- 1,2,3, relax*. Then repeat the freeze adding speaking thoughts spoken by the characters themselves in turn or other children standing behind them to voice the thoughts.
- Repeat with another object unless they are all included in the first freeze.
- Either stop the drama at this point and move to the writing or develop the freeze-frames by asking the children if they would like to talk to the character by putting yourself in the hot-seat as teacher-in-role. If you choose the hot-seat then ask the children to predict what the character might say about the frozen moment and try to incorporate their ideas in what you say in the hot-seat. Use a scarf as a sign of role as well as sitting in a designated hot-seat chair.
- Use the ideas from the hot-seat to further develop the storyline if appropriate and look for opportunities for further writing.
- Ask the children to draw one of the freeze-frames with added thought bubbles and a sentence describing what is happening.
- Work with the children to help them compose their own poems about their special things and why they're special, write sentences about their own special things or write lists. Display these on the wall inside an outline of a box or make a real box called OUR SPECIAL THINGS to put the writing inside.

> **Extension activity**
>
> Children choose one to three objects that could be in a special box belonging to a story character e.g. Cinderella's special box or a mermaid's special box. They draw a large outline of the object and write about the object(s) inside.

d   DRAMATIC PLAY

Planning and resources

- Select a suitable context for all the class to play roles as a group. Choose a situation where the activities can easily be mimed e.g. servants in a castle helping to prepare for a royal event or party, a group of children packing to go on a camping or an adventure holiday or a group of astronauts setting off to explore a new planet.

You will need

- A hall or cleared space for the drama activity;
- A scarf as a sign of teacher-in-role if needed.

What to do

- Start the drama by asking children to pretend to be an imaginary group engaged in your chosen activity. Start with dramatic play as discussed in Chapter 7, but instead of posing

a problem after the activity, stop the drama and ask the children what they think might happen next to make a good story. Have a suggestion ready yourself if the children struggle to think of anything to give them an idea of possibilities. Make a list of ideas, if necessary, and then ask the class to select one idea.
- Select an appropriate drama strategy to depict or explore the children's chosen idea. This could be a frozen moment with thoughts, talking to a character via teacher-in-role, more dramatic play or an imaginary pathway where everyone describes one feature of the route. Try to focus the outcome of the drama strategies on a learning opportunity with a view to a writing task either there and then or at a later time in the classroom. For example, children may need to write out invitations to the royal event in the story or a list of essential equipment for the adventure holiday. Children enjoy having writing materials to hand at the edge of the drama space so they can write as the need arises but if this is not possible then you can spread the drama over more than one lesson to accommodate a pause for writing in the classroom. This arrangement is very flexible and depends on the ideas and your own circumstances.
- After the children have explored one or two ideas in drama, talk about how the story might end.
- Then tell the children the final version of their story in your own words, to add status. If you can record it to play again then that is the best option.
- Work with the class to write the final story or ask individuals to write parts of the story.

Extension activity

Plan out three to five key moments from the story as freeze-frames for a group of the children to depict and use them to share the story with others in an assembly. The class can write a sentence to go with each freeze-frame which they can read out during the assembly. If you have recorded the story then this might be something to include as well.

KEY STAGE TWO EXAMPLES

a   **THE KEY**

Planning and resources

You will need

- A key of some kind. You can use a small key for a locked box or diary or an old iron door key. A modern door key can also be used but this can be less intriguing for younger children;
- A space at the front of the class or a cleared space for the drama;
- A scarf as a sign of teacher-in-role if necessary.

What to do

- Show the children the key and tell them that it will form the basis of a story that they will first explore through drama and then write their own version or a class story.
- Explain that you will pass the key round and invite the person with the key to invent one fact about it. However, their fact cannot contradict what others have already said e.g. if one child says the key opens a red door, the next person cannot say the key opens a blue door unless they say it opens a blue as well as a red door. Tell the children that you will write down the facts as each child speaks, so they can remember what has already been said. Talk about possible facts like where the key was made, what it opened, who it belonged to, who used it, was it lost or found, is it old or a copy, etc. Children can also add a fact to another person's fact e.g. *a boy found the key on the grass* can be followed by *the boy took the key to school with him*.
- Give every child an opportunity to contribute a fact about the key but allow children to pass if they cannot think of anything. This can happen towards the end of the activity after several facts have already been mentioned. Return to those who passed after the activity to see if they have thought of anything.
- Look at the list of facts and ask the children to select any that they wish to explore further. For example, they may choose the moment the key turned a diary lock. Why was the diary locked? After inviting children to come up with some possible reasons, choose a drama strategy to explore it further. For example, you can ask a confident pair of children to create a short improvised scene for the class showing when the character told someone about their diary to reveal why it was so secret. You can ask pairs to improvise their own scenes and report back to the class and/or invite a few to share their improvisations or invite a child to take the role of the diary owner in the hot-seat. You can use teacher-in-role to play the parent or friend of the diary owner and talk about how secretive they are or how you may try to find the key to take a look.
- Once the ideas have been explored, organise the children into groups to select one moment from the story of the key. They should then make a freeze-frame with a caption and thoughts or a short improvised scene of the moment.
- Allow groups to share their drama work before asking individuals to write their group's work as a narrative, poem, playscript or a page in a graphic novel.

> **Extension activity**
>
> Children imagine the key was in a museum and write a page of information for the display.

b   DIRECTING THE STORY

This involves children making decisions out of role about the next part of the drama and the direction they wish to take it in order to create an interesting story. This is later written as a whole class story or parts of the story are written by individuals. There can also be writing opportunities within the make-up of the story.

Planning and resources

Select a suitable context for an imaginary community as discussed in Chapter 8, but instead of planning a problem, think about some possible ways forward that the children might want to take and consider some appropriate drama strategies. This will depend on what the children say, but you will have some ideas for plan B if the children are stuck for ideas.

You will need

- A hall or cleared space for the drama;
- A few small items of clothing in case you work as teacher-in-role.

What to do

- Start off the imaginary community as discussed in Chapter 8, which usually involves some kind of dramatic play.
- Stop the drama and ask the children what they think should happen next to make the drama into an interesting story. Ask them to talk in small groups before collecting their ideas and then discuss and take a vote to decide on the next step. The children decide on the direction but you will need to decide what that looks like in terms of a drama strategy. Try to select one that will involve some kind of exploration or provide information that will move the story forward. Also, try to look for opportunities for writing where you could pause the drama to return to the classroom for the writing and then pick up the story again in the drama for the next lesson.
- Repeat the above as many times as is appropriate to conclude the story.
- Either work with the children or ask the children to produce parts of their story or ask individuals or pairs to write a story map of the events.

Extension activity

Children create a series of freeze-frames with captions to represent illustrations of key moments in their story.

Conclusion

I hope the ideas in this book will encourage more teachers to use drama to support the teaching of writing in the primary school. Whether teachers use it as a helping hand in the classroom or as a compelling context, drama has the potential not just to motivate writing but to improve the quality and integrity of the work. Based on my own teaching and that of others, I'm in no doubt that drama can make a significant contribution to the teaching of writing. With this in mind, I conclude this book with some references to children's writing that I have collected over the years, mostly sent to me by teachers after working with them in drama. All the teachers remarked on how the drama experience had had a positive impact, not just on the motivation to write but on the quality and imagination of the children.

Year 6: Refugees from Volcano Island have been given shelter by another Island community but all is not well

> Child 1 wrote a letter of complaint as a resident of Volcano Island. They are grateful to the island for letting them stay, but at the same time, they are disgusted with the way they are treated. They have to live in a barn and work in a factory.

> Child 2 wrote that they were disgusted with the place they are living in. They are in a barn which is damp and freezing cold....The boss of the factory says they are not allowed out of the building because they are from Volcano Island and might cause bother. But they are still grateful for having somewhere to sleep and food to eat.

Year 5: Children in role as inhabitants of Hamlyn write to the newspaper after meeting the mayor

> One child wrote that they are still having rats in their houses. They've tried everything. They all made traps, but there were too many rats. One rat tried to bite a baby. They went to the mayor, but so far he has done nothing.

Year 4: A drama about Theseus and Ariadne. Children were in role as the young people who accompanied Theseus

A child wrote that the best bit was where they had to get all the food for the journey and when Prince Theseus killed the Minototaur when he chopped its head off. They also liked the pretending sword and the casket.

Year 3: Open-ended drama – Ways to test for a dragon on arriving on an island with a volcano

Two boys offered to solve the problem in the following way: get some water and if a dragon comes out they will chuck water all over its head and then escape on the boat.

Year 2: Back in time in a spaceship to Isaac Newton's farm as part of a topic on gravity

A child wrote about how they liked the bit when they were moving very slowly as it was very relaxing. They were very excited when they started. Their favourite bit was when they camouflaged the spaceship and learnt not to mess with time and learnt about gravity.

Another child wrote about how they wished they could see the real Isaac Newton.

Year 1: Helping Daddy Bear

A child wrote about how they liked mopping the floor. They wrote about how Goldilocks made a big mess and Daddy Bear was happy with the help the children gave him.

Year 1: Drama about a parcel delivered to Granny Grey by mistake

All the children from one class wanted to write a letter to Granny Grey because she loves letters and doesn't get many. One child mentioned that they were practising writing letters and have their own school Christmas stamps. Everyone was glad that Granny Grey wasn't too sad at the end.

One child explained that they had a drama about Miss Grey and Miss Green. The postman delivered a parcel to the wrong house. It was Granny Grey's birthday and she thought it was a present from her daughter.

Another child explained that the new postman delivered a parcel to the wrong house. It was only his second day. It was supposed to go to Mrs Green's daughter. She was crying in the bedroom. Mrs Grey said she was sorry.

I conclude with an example of another short letter sent to Granny Grey after the drama with Year 1, telling Granny Grey that they had three gerbils and that the gerbils were really funny.

Aside from making me smile at the irrelevance (there were no pets or gerbils in the drama), it shows that even a compelling drama can take children in a completely different direction! So when asking children to write in relation to a drama, be prepared for the unexpected.

Drama strategies

The following drama strategies are arranged in alphabetical order and have been selected based on their potential to support the teaching of writing. They include other strategies not mentioned in this book and most of the well-known, tried and tested approaches to drama, but they do not represent a comprehensive list. Suggestions on how to make the best use of the strategies have been added to the definitions where appropriate.

Drama is made up of a number of different strategies to be selected according to the learning objectives and the needs of the children. Whilst many of the strategies are useful as one-off classroom activities, they are most effective when incorporated into a sustained whole group drama experience.

Actions

An abstract way of portraying real-life everyday activities and events, actions can be mimed or accompanied by sounds or speech. They can also be a way of expressing abstract concepts such as scientific processes or geographical features as part of an embodied approach to learning. Their function in the context of drama-in-education is to build belief in an imaginary context or encourage thoughtful consideration and expression of meaning rather than producing an accurate theatrical performance. They also offer a tangible experience from which to write.

Action/Freeze narration

Best suited to children in Years R to 4, Action/Freeze Narration allows all the children to physically re-enact a sequence of events according to the teacher's narration. Children mime the actions individually but, alongside each other, all playing the same character following the same narration. The events are presented in sequential sections with the children miming the actions on the word *Action* and stopping on the word *Freeze* each time. Whilst this activity requires careful listening during the narration, it involves a discussion between each section on what happens next and how best to portray the characters and events.

Character circle

Originally employed by actors to explore relationships between one of the main characters and the other characters in a play, the Character Circle can be adapted to enable children to examine relationships in stories or plays where there are several characters. Each child or group is assigned to a different character in the story, other than the main character. Children are given time to decide how their character feels about the main character based on what they know of the text. The children sit in a circle around an empty chair representing the main character to share their views. Another version is to ask a confident child to sit in the chair as the main character, to respond to what the other characters say. This is useful for writing character studies, roles on the wall or diaries.

Communal voice

Two groups represent the individual voices of two different characters in conversation. The two groups stand opposite each other. When one of the groups speaks, they take on the role of their assigned character, using the words *I* and *me* whenever they speak. Different children in the group take turns to represent the voice of their character, but each contributor must pick up and continue the thread of the conversation. Communal Voice helps children explore characters' motives, feelings and relationships at significant moments in a story, but it can also link to topics and information texts. For example, a modern character can talk to a historical character or to someone living in another geographical area and creatures can hold imaginary conversations about habitats or climate change. Useful for writing dialogue or playscripts.

Conscience alley/decision alley/conscience forest

In conscience alley, the class is divided into two groups to represent two conflicting, polarised sides of an argument or point of view. When used to develop reading for meaning, the arguments are usually based on a fictional character facing a dilemma or issues in a non-fiction text. Children are often asked to represent arguments from the text which may not align with their own views. Where this is the case, they should be given an opportunity to express their own views after the activity. In the traditional conscience alley, the two opposing sides face each other in two lines to form an alleyway or corridor. A child or teacher-in-role as a character walks slowly between the two lines as if walking down the alley. Children speak to the character as they walk down the alley, presenting pre-prepared reasoned arguments to try to persuade them of their given point of view. The character can walk down one side of the alleyway to hear one side of the argument and then back along the opposite side to hear the other side or walk down the centre listening to alternate views.

Conscience alley can be adapted to become an imaginary public debate or trial in which some children take on roles to present two polarised points of view, whilst others vote or play the part of a jury. Useful for writing balanced arguments.

Another version of conscience alley is conscience forest where a character's confused thoughts are revealed in a dream. In this version, the children stand like trees in a tangled forest rather than in an alley. The character walks among the children, who whisper the character's inner thoughts. This version can be used in a classroom with children sitting at desks.

Dreamscapes

Children use keywords and phrases from the text to create a dream sequence. It's often used to demonstrate how words can evoke menacing moods in poems, novels and plays. There are many ways to produce a dream sequence, ranging from an audio recording of keywords and phrases to a physical interpretation such as a version of conscience forest. There is also an option to combine the words with music and dance.

Echo

The Echo is designed to improve an actor's performance by delivering lines or reciting a text. It focuses mainly on developing the skills of clarity, audibility and confidence when performing to an audience. The reader reads one of their lines to the rest of the group, who then echo it so the performer has a sense of how an audience might hear and receive it. It works best if the teacher models the process, making deliberate mistakes for the children to identify e.g. reading too quietly, with head down, timidly, etc.

Forum theatre

The whole class/group (the forum) works with the teacher to direct a small group improvisation as it takes place. It can be adapted to enable a class of children to direct and produce an authentic freeze-frame based on a text, which can then be written up as eyewitness accounts.

Freeze

Children take up a frozen position, usually in character. The effect is similar to a pause in a video clip. Freezing characters can slow down the action to facilitate discussion and reflection on the text, as well as provide a means to pause or stop the drama. This slows down the action to focus on more depth.

Freeze-frames (Tableaux or Still Image)

A small group of children physically depicts a significant moment from a text by freezing the action, as if in a frame. The freeze-frames are usually shown to the rest of the class. When combined with forum theatre, freeze-frames are an effective way to enable observation, investigation and analysis of a text by the whole class. They support reading for meaning by developing the skills of inference and deduction and encouraging empathy and support writing by adding a written element to the frame or recording the event as an eyewitness. Illustrations and photos in books can also be used as a stimulus for a freeze-frame and children can create freeze-frames to represent their own ideas for illustrations. Freeze-frames have a wide range of uses including making a sequenced storyboard with multiple freeze-frames and captions, expressing predictions and forming a basis for improvised dialogue when brought to life. This can also be a valuable way for groups to represent the main ideas in information texts, such as the digestive system, gravity and the solar system, where they use their bodies in a more abstract way to provide evidence of their understanding.

Guided tour

One child leads a partner on an imaginary guided tour around the setting of a story. It can be based on an illustration, a map or a written description. Roles are then reversed to travel back. Alternatively, the teacher leads all the children on an imaginary guided tour to describe the setting. This activity works best as a physical tour with the children walking around the room. If space is limited, children can sit with their eyes closed as the teacher describes the setting as if they were walking through it. This can form the basis for a written piece on the setting after the drama.

Hot-seating

A person or a group takes on a role when sitting on a designated chair or seat, in order to answer questions. Hot-seating can be a powerful tool in helping children to empathise with characters or gain a deeper understanding of the consequences of events in a text. It can also bring children closer to the text by offering different perspectives, bringing the events alive through the eyes of the characters. It can be applied to non-fiction texts allowing children to ask questions of animals, birds, sea life and insects.

Consider the most appropriate character for the hot-seat in relation to your objectives. The protagonist in a story may not be the best one to challenge the thinking of the group. In some stories, the main character may prove so unpopular that it would be difficult for the children to respond without prejudice or they may react in an extreme manner. In some cases, it may be better to hot-seat a minor or invented character who could answer questions about the main character, such as a neighbour, relative or friend. There are versions of hot-seating involving groups rather than individuals, but whatever form it takes, hot-seating relies on the knowledge and understanding of those in the hot-seat, so preparation is required if children are to take on this role instead of the teacher.

Hot-seating can provide opportunities for children to develop their questioning skills but often need support to devise appropriately focused questions. This provides an opportunity for children to consider questions in relation to audience and purpose and to write questions as part of a factual book.

Improvisations

There are two different types of improvisations: Spontaneous and Polished.

1. In *Spontaneous* Improvisation, children talk in role without preparation, often in pairs or small groups. The improvisations can be performed by one group in front of an audience or several groups can improvise simultaneously without an audience. Sometimes the groups stop to listen to snippets of each other's improvisations (see Spotlighting).
2. *Polished* Improvisations are planned and rehearsed before they are shared.

Both kinds of improvisations can be reworked and rehearsed to form the basis of a written scripted performance or a script for others to perform.

Whilst improvisations allow children the freedom to express themselves in role, the content should always be in line with school values.

Letters from characters

Children are sent imaginary letters from characters asking them for help, advice or information. They can also provide new information to move the drama on and the audience and purpose for replying in writing.

Line up

Children representing characters are lined up by the class on a continuum from the highest to the lowest, according to given criteria. Discussion arises from the need for whole class agreement or as a response to a line up made by an individual child or the teacher. Characters can be lined up according to criteria such as their status within the setting, from the kindest to the cruellest, the most influential to the least influential and even the most popular to the least popular with the class, etc. Placing the more minor characters on the continuum in relation to each other can provoke valuable in-depth discussion. Character studies of minor characters can be written up after this drama.

Mantle-of-the-expert

The term 'Mantle-of-the-Expert' was used by the drama-in-education pioneer Dorothy Heathcote in the 1970s, to describe the technique where children take on the roles and responsibilities of experts, commissioned by someone to undertake an important task. The roles are often those of professionals such as architects, historians, museum curators and designers and can involve researching information from non-fiction texts.

Children move in and out of the drama to perform the tasks, seek more information and reflect or solve problems. The teacher usually works in role alongside the children with equal power and authority during the drama. The term comes from the idea of throwing expertise onto the shoulders of the children like a mantle or a cloak. It is used in many schools as a key approach to teaching and learning alongside other strategies.

In this book, the Mantle-of-the-Expert strategy has been adapted and extended to include any roles where children are in a position to give others help and advice, whether written or verbal.

Meet and Greet

Working in role, children move around the space in pairs, meeting other pairs to share information linked to the context of the drama. After the activity, children share what they have discovered. The focus of this strategy is on listening and gathering information to feed into the dramatic context, but it can provide a reason to write role cards or character descriptions in preparation for this activity.

Object game

Children imagine they are objects in a setting, describing what they might see, feel and sense without naming the object. Others try to guess which object they are describing, then discuss how the object came to be there and why they think the author included it. Objects can include other non-human things such as animals, insects, birds, plants, buildings, etc. Children can then write their own descriptions of objects.

Pathway

This is similar to conscience alley where children arrange themselves to form a pathway for a character or a visitor to travel through. However, in the Pathway strategy, the children describe what the traveller might see or sense as they walk along. This can be a written sentence or verbally expressed. Children can organise themselves to create a winding path or use their bodies to form features for the traveller to negotiate e.g. pairs join hands to form an arch for the traveller to walk under or groups make an obstacle for them to step over or around. This strategy is a useful way to examine and recreate aspects of a setting in a text and is sometimes used in conjunction with the Guided Tour strategy.

Playscripts

A playscript is a written text designed to become a theatrical performance. Theatre is organic and involves a team effort with all the separate elements working together to tell a story. Playscripts written for whole school productions provide large numbers of children with a valuable and memorable theatrical experience, whereas shorter classroom playscripts or single scenes from longer plays provide more opportunities to focus on reading for meaning via the medium of a script. The need to read and perform lines with appropriate expression, either individually or chorally, provides children with an opportunity to extend their vocabulary by considering the meaning and significance of keywords and phrases in a shared text. Short playscripts designed for single classes of children include historical, environmental and scientific topics, adaptations of novels and melodramatic versions of Shakespeare and classic stories. Some plays are based on characters from reading schemes and include versions of traditional stories.

Puppet-in-role

Younger children find puppets engaging and are only too willing to help them solve problems within a story. Puppet-in-role works best with a glove puppet or one that can be manipulated to indicate emotions. They can be a useful introduction to stories with animal or fantasy characters, but the puppet does not have to be the main character. You can invent a role for the puppet such as a concerned friend of the main character or someone who might have witnessed the problems and wants to solve them. The puppet usually communicates by whispering to the teacher, who relays what has been said to the children, thus avoiding the need to be a ventriloquist. Finding the puppet in a sad or confused state increases the children's level of engagement but it's important to maintain the puppet's responses throughout the activity, because in the child's mind making the puppet feel better is the main objective. Children can also provide written advice or a book of how to do whatever the puppet is struggling with.

Puppets on sticks

Stick puppets representing specific characters provide younger children with an opportunity to wave their puppets whenever their character speaks during a story reading. They can also join in with any repeated words or refrains spoken by their character. They also help children identify passages of direct speech during a reading.

Role-on-the-wall

This strategy has its roots in the character analysis employed by actors to gain greater insights into characters' motivations, but it can be adapted to enable children to explore characters in a text. In order to create a Role-On-The-Wall, children are encouraged to collect information and formulate opinions about a character, with close reference to the text. The activity involves drawing a large outline of the character or characters on a wall or screen. Children discuss and add information about the character to the outline, based on what they know of the text and how they respond to it. The criteria for what is collected and recorded can vary according to the focus of the learning. The information displayed can be added to or changed as children read more of the text, thus supporting discussions on character profiles, character development, relationships with other characters and authorial intent. Children can also write their own role outlines in their books in the same way.

Silent movie

This is a light-hearted activity designed to provide a quick overview of a plot or sequence of events. It works best with older children in Years 5-6. Children walk through the events of a whole plot or part of a plot, performing the appropriate actions according to the teacher's narration. They move briskly in a similar manner to a silent movie, but not artificially speeded up. Some children play the characters, whilst others keep up the pace by ushering the actors into the correct scenes at the right times or keeping a check on the procedures as the audience. The first run-through needs to be a rehearsal, with the second attempt being a performance without any prompts or checks. The silent movie strategy is particularly useful with complicated plots, but it can also be used to illustrate sequences in non-fiction texts such as instructions, historical events or sequences in science. Children also enjoy the challenge of writing part of a well-known story or their own story as a silent movie.

Sound effects

Interrogating the text to identify and create appropriate sound effects for a poem or story helps children consider those explicit and implicit auditory aspects of a text that contribute to the meaning. The sounds can be created with instruments, voices and/or objects. These can be added to any scripted work written by the class or individuals.

Soundscapes/sound collages/sound machines

This is a more sophisticated version of creating sound effects. It involves the creation of a collage of sounds to paint a picture of the setting, atmosphere or theme of a story or topic and can be combined with dance and movement. Using words from the text, voices and percussion, it can also be presented as an imaginary Sound Machine that repeats on a loop until switched off. Keywords can be repeated or overlapped to emphasise their significance and increase their impact. The strategy presents an opportunity for children to explore how an author uses words and events to create different moods, atmospheres and suspense.

Spotlighting/over-heard conversations

Spotlighting or Over-Heard Conversations take place whilst groups are improvising spontaneously without an audience. The teacher freezes the action and shines an imaginary spotlight on each group in turn, allowing everyone else to listen in to a snippet of their improvised conversation. Only the group under the spotlight is active. The rest of the class remains silent as an audience.

Spotlighting has the potential to create a deeper understanding of characters and events in texts. Whilst developing speaking and listening through collaborative group work, spotlighting enables all children to perform a short piece of improvisation in whatever way they feel comfortable, with an option to convert their snippets into written playscripts or character studies.

Another version of an Over-Heard Conversation is where the children listen in to the teacher-in-role having an imaginary telephone conversation related to a story. The children listening in have to work out who the character is, where they are, what they are talking about and who they might be talking to. The telephone conversation is conducted by a teacher-in-role in order to present a degree of challenge that encourages further exploration of the story, but older or more confident children can provide similar conversations for others to guess.

Suspense alley

This is presented in a similar way to conscience alley, but without a dilemma. Children identify the words and phrases used by an author to create suspense in a particular extract from a novel. The words are shared out amongst the children who stand roughly in the order in which they appear in the text, to form two lines like an alley. A child or teacher-in-role as the main character walks slowly through the alley as the children call out their words to reveal the developing suspense. Children can experiment with their own suspense words to create a poem or a short piece of writing.

Teacher-in-role/adult-in-role

Teacher-in-role, as the term suggests, involves the teacher taking on a role as part of a drama activity. It provides a model of appropriate language and behaviour for role-playing and can present alternative perspectives and challenges within the dramatic context. A teacher-in-role can drive a narrative forward, build tension and provide or request key information in response to the particular needs of the children.

It enables a teacher to both challenge and support children from inside the drama, allowing the teacher to co-construct powerful learning environments, where children can gain deeper insights into the meanings of texts and are given clear audience and purpose for writing.

(See Introduction: managing the drama).

Teacher narrator

The teacher acts as a narrator within a drama activity, pausing the process to link key moments, move time on, introduce information or introduce themselves as a teacher-in-role or present a challenge. The narration also models appropriate story language and structure.

Thought-tracking

On a signal from the teacher, children in role speak their character's thoughts aloud at a given moment in the drama. Where children are playing themselves within an imaginary situation, their thoughts will represent their own responses to that situation. These can be represented in writing via thought bubbles.

Where do you stand now?/the Spider's Web

Whilst technically not a drama strategy, Where Do You Stand Now? is frequently used as part of a drama activity to give children an opportunity to reflect on the issues, characters or events and write a balanced argument. Each corner or area of the room represents a different opinion. You can place cards at opposite sides of the room saying YES and NO, AGREE and DISAGREE or cards with statements on in different areas. Children choose to stand in the area that best represents their opinions at that moment in time. Those who are undecided must stand either in a central area or closer to one area than another, but need to be prepared to justify their choice. Children move on the word Go and some are then asked to explain their choices. The activity is often repeated to allow children an opportunity to revise their original opinions after listening to the views of others.

In the Spider's Web version, someone stands in the centre of a circle to read out a statement. The person can read out the statement in role or as themselves. On the word *Go*, the children in the circle move to stand closer or further away from the person, representing a web of opinions indicating how far they agree or disagree with the statement.

Whole group drama

In whole group drama, both the children and the teacher enter the same imaginary context, moving through the narrative, behaving and reacting as if it were really happening. It is sometimes referred to as Living Through or Process drama. Whole group drama can be paused in order to use other drama strategies to deepen the experience or paused for longer periods to carry out related research or written work. When combined with teacher-in-role, whole group drama is the most effective of all the drama strategies. Through taking part in an imagined experience that feels real, children develop an emotional engagement with the drama. Whole group drama blurs the boundaries between the text and the reader as children share an experience from inside a story. It also provides a compelling context for writing.

Basic whole group drama usually has three stages, working in a similar way to a basic story structure:

1 Set up and build belief in the imaginary context.
2 Set a problem or task within the imaginary context and allow the children to respond.
3 Reflect on the experience out of role.

Further reading and resources

Baldwin, P. and John, R. (2012) **INSPIRING WRITING THROUGH DRAMA AGES 7-16.** Bloomsbury.
Heathcote, D. and Bolton, G. (1995) **DRAMA FOR LEARNING.** Heinemann.
Taylor, T. (2016) **A BEGINNER'S GUIDE TO MANTLE OF THE EXPERT.** Singular Publishing.
Wagner, B. J. (1999) **DOROTHY HEATHCOTE: DRAMA AS A LEARNING MEDIUM.** Calendar Islands.

Websites

mantleoftheexpert.com

Texts

Ahlberg, A. (1984) **DOG IN THE PLAYGROUND (Please Mrs Butler).** Puffin.
Ahlberg, J. and Ahlberg, A. (1999) **THE JOLLY POSTMAN.** Puffin.
Anderson, S. (2020) **THE CASTLE OF TANGLED MAGIC.** Usborne.
Armitage, R. and D. (1977) **THE LIGHTHOUSE KEEPER'S LUNCH.** Scholastic.
Balen, K. (2021) **OCTOBER, OCTOBER.** Bloomsbury.
Baxter, N. (2011) **THE THREE LITTLE PIGS.** Ladybird.
Bradley, M. (2021) **BUMBLE AND SNUG AND THE ANGRY PIRATES.** Hodder.
Brown, J. (2017) **FLAT STANLEY: STANLEY IN SPACE.** Egmont.
Browne, A. (1994) **ZOO.** Red Fox.
Bunzl, P. (2016) **COGHEART.** Usborne.
Bunzl, P. (2020) **SHADOWSEA.** Usborne.
Bunzl, P. (2021) **FEATHERLIGHT.** Barrington Stoke.
Butler, S. (2018) **DOG DIARIES.** Penguin.
Campion, K. (2020) **THE LAST POST.** Troubador.
Carney, E. (2016) **CATS VERSUS DOGS.** National Geographic Children's Books.
Carter, J. (2021) **WEIRD WILD AND WONDERFUL.** Otter-Barry.
Clanton, B. (2019) **NARWHAL UNICORN OF THE SEA.** Egmont.
Clarke, P. (2008) **MY NAME IS...** (The Booktime Book of Fantastic First Poems Ed. Crebbin, J.). Puffin.
Cousins, L. (2020) **LETTERS FROM MAISIE.** Candlewick Press.
Davidson, S. (2012) **GOLDILOCKS AND THE THREE BEARS.** Usborne.
Daywalt, D. and Jeffers, O. (2014) **THE DAY THE CRAYONS QUIT.** Harper Collins.
De la Bedoyere, C. (2015) **WOULD YOU RATHER: SHAKE LIKE A DOG OR CLIMB LIKE A CAT?** QED Publishing.
Di Camillo, K. (2018) **GOOD ROSIE.** Walker Books.
Donaldson, J. (2013) **PLAYTIME.** Macmillan.
Dorling Kindersley. (2021) **BEHIND THE SCENES AT THE ZOO.** D. K. Children's.
Edge, C. (2019) **THE LONGEST NIGHT OF CHARLIE MOON.** Nosy Crow.
Flor Ada, A. (1998) **YOURS TRULY, GOLDILOCKS.** Atheneum Books for Young Readers.

Ford, M. (2015) **THE IMAGINATION BOX.** Faber and Faber.
Foreman, M. (1972) **DINOSAURS AND ALL THAT RUBBISH.** Puffin.
George, R. (1976) **CHARLIE AND THE CHOCOLATE FACTORY – A PLAY.** Penguin.
George, R. (2017) **JAMES AND THE GIANT PEACH: THE PLAY.** Puffin.
Gliori, D. (1999) **NO MATTER WHAT.** Bloomsbury.
Gold, H. (2021) **THE LAST BEAR.** Harper Collins.
Goldberg-Sloan, H. and Wolitzer, M. (2019) **TO NIGHTOWL FROM DOGFISH.** Egmont.
Gravett, E. (2016) **MEERKAT MAIL.** Two Hoots.
Grill, W. (2014) **SHACKLETON'S JOURNEY.** Flying Eye Books.
Guarnaccia, S. (2010) **THE THREE LITTLE PIGS: AN ARCHITECTURAL TALE.** Abrams Books.
Harrison, L. S. (2021) **ANGEL'S CHILD.** Troubador.
Hedderwick, M. (2010) **KATY MORAG'S ISLAND STORIES.** Red Fox.
Henn, S. (2020) **PIZAZZ.** Simon & Schuster.
Horacek, P. (2019) **THE LAST TIGER.** Otter-Barry Books.
Hughes, S. (1999) **DOGGER.** Red Fox.
Husband, A. (2010) **DEAR TEACHER.** Source Books Inc.
Hutchins, P. (2002) **DON'T FORGET THE BACON.** Red Fox.
Hutchins, P. (2003) **ROSIE'S WALK.** Red Fox.
Hutchins, P. (2013) **WE'RE GOING ON A PICNIC.** Red Fox.
James, S. (2008) **THE WILD WOODS.** Walker Books.
James, S. (2016) **DEAR GREENPEACE.** Walker Books.
Jamieson, V. (2017) **ROLLER GIRL.** Puffin.
Johnson, P. (2005) **GET WRITING: AGES 4–7.** A&C Black.
Johnson, P. (2008) **GET WRITING: AGES 7–12.** A&C Black.
Keeping, C. and Crossley-Holland, K. (1995) **BEOWULF.** OUP.
Kinnear, N. (2020) **SHHH! QUIET.** Alison Green Books.
Kirtley, S. (2020) **THE WILD WAY HOME.** Bloomsbury.
Kuzniar, M. (2020) **THE SHIP OF SHADOWS.** Random House.
Lacey, J. (2018) **THE DRAGON SITTER'S SURPRISE.** Andersen Press.
Lacome, J. (1995) **WALKING THROUGH THE JUNGLE.** Walker Books.
Lear, E. Illustrated by Beck, I. (2002) **THE JUMBLIES.** Corgi.
Lonergan, O. (2020) **CATS' EYE VIEW OF … LITTER.** Nielson.
Magorian, M. (1983) **GOODNIGHT MISTER TOM.** Puffin.
Martin, J. (2002) **12 FABULOUSLY FUNNY FAIRY TALE PLAYS.** Scholastic.
McLachlan, J. (2019) **LAND OF ROAR.** Egmont.
Messenger, N. (2012) **THE LAND OF NEVERBELIEVE.** Walker Books.
Palmer, T. (2021) **ARCTIC STAR.** Barrington Stoke.
Parr, L. (2022) **WHEN THE WAR CAME HOME.** Bloomsbury.
Pearce, P. (2015) **TOM'S MIDNIGHT GARDEN.** OUP.
Petty, K. (2006) **THE PERFECT PUNCTUATION BOOK.** Bodley Head.
Reid, S. (2017) **FANTASTIC MR FOX: THE PLAY.** Puffin.
Robertson, D. (2018) **LIZZIE AND THE BIRDS.** Prim-Ed Publishing.
Robinson, H. (2017) **A SONG FOR WILL.** Strauss House.
Rosen, M. (1993) **WE'RE GOING ON A BEAR HUNT.** Walker Books.
Rosen, M. (2014) **SEND FOR A SUPER HERO.** Walker Books.
Rosen, M. (2016) **QUESTION MARK (Jelly Boots, Smelly Boots).** Bloomsbury.
Rosen, M. and Sharratt, N. (2012) **DEAR FAIRY GODMOTHER.** Walker Books.
Rumble, C. (2020) **RIDING A LION.** Troika Books.
Rumble, C. (2020) **THE INTERRUPTING FULL STOP (Riding a Lion).** Troika Books.
Said, S. F. (2003) **VARJAK PAW.** Corgi.
Seed, A. (2020) **INTERVIEW WITH A TIGER.** Welbeck.
Seed, A. (2021) **INTERVIEW WITH A SHARK.** Welbeck.
Selway, M. (1996) **WISH YOU WERE HERE.** Red Fox.
Sendak, M. (1992) **WHERE THE WILD THINGS ARE.** Harper Collins.
Simon, F. (2009) **HORRID HENRY EATS A VEGETABLE (Horrid Henry's Underpants).** Orion Children's Books.

Smart, J. (2021) **BUNNY VS MONKEY AND THE LEAGUE OF DOOM.** David Fickling Books.
Smouha, C. K. (2019) **ICED OUT.** Cicada Books Ltd.
Sorosiak, C. (2019) **I COSMO.** Nosy Crow.
Southgate, V. (2012) **LADYBIRD TALES: THE THREE BILLY GOATS GRUFF.** Ladybird.
Stanton, L. (2020) **TRICKY PUNCTUATION IN CARTOONS.** Jessica Kingsley.
Steinke, A. N. (2018) **MR WOLF'S CLASS.** Scholastic.
Stevens, G. (2021) **STELLA AND THE SEAGULL.** OUP.
Strathie, C. (2017) **DEAR DINOSAUR.** Scholastic.
Taylor, T. (2019) **MALAMANDER.** Walker Books.
Tomlinson, J. (1968) **THE OWL WHO WAS AFRAID OF THE DARK.** Egmont.
Truss, L. (2007) **THE GIRLS LIKE SPAGHETTI.** Putnam Publishing Group.
Waddell, M. (1991) **FARMER DUCK.** Walker Books.
Waddell, M. (1995) **THE BIG BAD MOLE'S COMING.** Walker Books.
Willems, M. (2020) **THE PIGEON SERIES.** Walker Books.
Wilson, A. (2021) **LIGHTNING FALLS.** Macmillan.
Wood, D. (2009) **DANNY CHAMPION OF THE WORLD: PLAYS FOR CHILDREN.** Puffin.
Wood, D. (2009) **THE BFG: PLAYS FOR CHILDREN.** Puffin.
Wood, D. (2017) **THE TWITS: THE PLAYS.** Puffin.
Wood, D. (2017) **THE WITCHES: THE PLAYS.** Puffin.
Yarlett, E. (2018) **DRAGON POST.** Walker Books.
Yarlett, E. (2019) **BEASTFEAST.** Walker Books.
Zetter, N. (2016) **ODD SOCKS.** Troika Books.

For Product Safety Concerns and Information please contact our EU
representative GPSR@taylorandfrancis.com
Taylor & Francis Verlag GmbH, Kaufingerstraße 24, 80331 München, Germany

www.ingramcontent.com/pod-product-compliance
Lightning Source LLC
Chambersburg PA
CBHW080225170426
43192CB00015B/2756